Saving My Assassin is gripping.

JERRY B. JENKINS
New York Times Bestselling Author

Saving My Assassin is a stirring account of valor under an oppressive regime and faith in the face of faithlessness. Prodan's heartbreaking, inspiring life journey will move readers of every background and serves as a call to action for a new generation of Americans. Through persecution, conversion, exile, and triumph, Virginia Prodan reminds us: there is always hope.

JIM DeMINT
Former Senator; President and CEO, The Heritage Foundation

Saving My Assassin is explosive! It is a celebration of awe-inspiring bravery filled with unforgettable moments! Virginia's courage to stand up for her beliefs and for others in the face of death serves as an encouragement to those of us who strive to do the same! She is a heroine of our time—a strong woman with a strong message. Virginia's memoir motivates you to discover not only the courage in you and the power of your voice, but also the purpose for your life! Everyone should read *Saving My Assassin*—a message that will stay with you long after the last chapter ends!

ED MARTIN
President, Eagle Forum

Virginia Prodan stood fearlessly against an oppressive Communist regime and the lawless leadership of Nicolai Ceauşescu. She chose to obey God rather than man and changed the course of history! Virginia mastered her fear of earthly consequences for the glory of God and now inspires her readers. Beyond inspiration, *Saving My Assassin* is a call to action: to live above fear—and to witness the miraculous. I believe this is the message for this generation of believers: we must rise above the fear of man to see a miraculous move of God.

TONY PERKINS
President, Family Research Council, Washington, DC

Saving My Assassin by Virginia Prodan is an amazing testimony of one woman's experience against oppression of faith and how she found the courage to stand strong in the face of insurmountable odds. More than that, there are lessons from Virginia's story on how we might lean on Jesus and his Word in the Scriptures to overcome our challenges . . . and potential dangers.

DAVID CURRY
CEO, Open Doors USA

Saving My Assassin is an extraordinary book! A truly courageous woman, Virginia Prodan—a lawyer and defender of the Christian faith who risked her life in one of the most brutal regimes of modern history. Her faith was forged in the furnace; it brought regular arrests, beatings, and death threats. Yet she never lost her courage or faith in God. Her story is an encouragement for Christians everywhere, called to stand—and perhaps die—for their faith.

JOSEPH P. INFRANCO
Senior Counsel and Vice President, Alliance Defending Freedom

Virginia Prodan's electrifying true story—*Saving My Assassin*—reads like a well-crafted novel but burns with the power only truth can convey—and in a very personal way. America is not Ceauşescu's Romania, but too many of our countrymen treat liberty casually, and some have traded their liberties for a mess of pottage. May God use Virginia's story to stir Americans to take a stand for the liberty so many of our fathers, mothers, brothers, and sisters have died to preserve.

REV. PIERRE BYNUM
Family Research Council Chaplain & National Prayer Director

Saving My Assassin is captivating, and you won't be able to put it down. Virginia Prodan has written an incredible book that every American will want to read. It's rare to find a book so well written and so emotionally powerful and yet teaching wonderful lessons about freedom and courage and the great moral principles to which we all need to aspire. This is a must-read.

KELLY SHACKELFORD, ESQ.
President, CEO, and Chief Counsel of Liberty Institute

Saving My Assassin is a riveting true story of a young woman standing for Christ in a government that would rather have her dead. It's not only entertaining, but Virginia's story provides the kind of inspiration and example that you may need as our world continues to darken.

> **DR. FRANK TUREK**
> Award-Winning Author and Coauthor;
> President of CrossExamined.org

How would you respond to a man sent to murder you? Hopefully, most Americans will never face that challenge, but Virginia Prodan has and lived to tell about it. *Saving My Assassin* is the story of a woman, standing for freedom during Romanian dictator Nicolae Ceauşescu's regime, who discovered that faith, hope, and love can overcome fear, bitterness, and hatred. Her real life so far has been a journey worthy of a Hollywood thriller. She has already proven that the American way of truth and justice can win. More important, though, she warns that our nation has stumbled onto a path destined for the darkness she escaped. Read Virginia's book to be inspired. Read this book to learn how to keep America free.

> **KEVIN D. FREEMAN, CFA**
> *New York Times* Bestselling Author of *Secret Weapon*

Saving My Assassin is an extraordinary, uplifting story of a human rights attorney who brought down the cruel dictator of Romania. Virginia Prodan is an inspiration to us and a reminder of the great promise of America.

MICHAEL A. NEEDHAM
Chief Executive Officer, Heritage Action for America

Saving My Assassin is a riveting, authoritative, and inspirational book! Virginia Prodan enlightens us not only about her fight under persecution but also about the real aspect of the infamous current war on Christians and how to win this war. *Saving My Assassin* will reach and define many generations. Everyone will treasure it. Virginia Prodan encourages us to find and to act upon the truth, the source of her incredible moral courage in the face of monstrous evil.

DR. JIM GARLOW
Senior Pastor, Skyline Wesleyan Church

Virginia Prodan's book, *Saving My Assassin*, is a relevant read: the story of a Christian attorney fighting for religious liberty against persecution. We are seeing growing persecution against the Judeo-Christian faith heritage and individual religious freedom here in America. Virginia's book tells her story—one of being strong and of good courage.

LIEUTENANT COLONEL ALLEN B. WEST (US ARMY, RETIRED)
President/CEO, National Center for Policy Analysis;
Member of 112th US Congress

Liberty and *freedom* are words that have lost some context in our American culture today. Virginia Prodan's life story encourages people to stand up for truth and their beliefs, despite the adversity and the cost. *Saving My Assassin* is a must-read for all as a reminder that freedom comes with a cost.

CHAD HENNINGS
Author; Former Defensive Tackle for the Air Force Academy Falcons and Dallas Cowboys; Winner of 3 Super Bowls

Virginia's riveting story of courage and faith is a great reminder of how precious freedom truly is and why it is so important to have those like Virginia willing to fight for that freedom in the courtroom and also the halls of our legislatures. *Saving My Assassin* also serves as a warning to all Americans that the brutality of tyranny often begins with the abuse of the judiciary, all while singing the praises of the rule of law.

RICK GREEN
Former Legislator; Author of *Constitution Alive!*

Reading Virginia Prodan's *Saving My Assassin* inspires faithful Christian witness in the face of systems of government and structures of power. Virginia offers real-life inspiration for intensifying obedience to our Lord Christ in today's public spaces. The One who transcends history and geography, controls politics and economics, and creates all peoples and nations will provide courage for us to persevere, and he will turn potential defeats to providential victories.

RAMESH RICHARD, PHD, THD
Professor, Dallas Theological Seminary; President, RREACH

Intriguing and life-changing! *Saving My Assassin* is a story of faith and courage that will open your eyes to the real and widespread persecution Christians face around the world. It chronicles the life-journey of attorney Virginia Prodan as she bravely fought against the anti-Christian government system in Romania and now in her adopted country, America. Although it reads like a novel, it is a true account of her fascinating and risky work. Reading her story will encourage you to stand firm in your faith and live boldly for Christ.

KAROL LADD
Bestselling Author of *The Power of a Positive Woman*

Saving My Assassin is the inspirational read of 2016, studded with invaluable life lessons of faith and resilience garnered on Virginia Prodan's incredible, historic journey. Virginia sounds the clarion call for Christians today everywhere! A terrific page turner.

NICK ADAMS
Bestselling Author & Commentator

I have listened raptly many times to my friend Virginia Prodan tell bits and pieces of her life's journey from the repression of Communist Romania to the liberty of America. It's an extraordinary, harrowing, and uplifting story. I'm thrilled she has put the entire story together in *Saving My Assassin*. Beyond creating a compelling read, she offers readers a potent affirmation of the power of unwavering faith and a standard for the kind of bravery needed in the world today to face down the many forms of tyranny plaguing freedom-loving people around the world.

DEBBIE GEORGATOS
Author; Radio Host of *Ladies, Can We Talk?*

Only someone who has experienced the tyranny and oppression of Communism can fully embrace the liberating joy of democracy. Virginia Prodan knows such joy and lives it out daily. As an international human rights attorney, Virginia has become a consummate freedom fighter. Hers is the inspiring story of escaping Communist Romania, being granted political asylum by the United States, becoming an American citizen, and now advocating for immigrants who desire to come to the United States legally. I am humbled to be Virginia's friend and honored to be her pastor. Not only is her story riveting, but her dramatic and graphic writing style will capture your mind and heart and will not let you go. Just wait: from the introduction on, you'll be hooked.

DR. JEFF WARREN
Senior Pastor, Park Cities Baptist Church, Dallas, Texas

Saving My Assassin will grab your heart from the very start and pull you from a dark pit of hellish discouragement to the lofty ramparts of a hope fulfilled. This book is a lightning bolt of truth that sends out a thunderclap warning for all today. Not defeated by raw fear nor circumstances unimaginable, this brave woman survived it all to find her name forever etched in the halls of heroic accomplishment. A must-read that will definitely inspire all that take this incredible journey.

BOB CORNUKE
Author

Virginia Prodan's love for America is palpable. *Saving My Assassin* will convince you that preserving American superpower serves not only her citizens, but also impacts countless lives around the globe that are enslaved by Marxism.

CATHIE ADAMS
President, Texas Eagle Forum

SAVING MY ASSASSIN

A MEMOIR BY VIRGINIA PRODAN

Tyndale House Publishers
Carol Stream, Illinois

Visit Tyndale online at tyndale.com.

TYNDALE and Tyndale's quill logo are registered trademarks of Tyndale House Publishers.

Saving My Assassin

Designed by Julie Chen and Jennifer Ghionzoli

Edited by Jane Vogel

Published in association with literary agent Tawny Johnson of D.C. Jacobson & Associates LLC, an Author Management Company. www.dcjacobson.com.

For information about special discounts for bulk purchases, please contact Tyndale House Publishers at csresponse@tyndale.com, or call 1-800-323-9400.

Library of Congress Cataloging-in-Publication Data
Names: Prodan, Virginia, author.
Title: Saving my assassin / Virginia Prodan.
Description: Carol Stream, IL : Tyndale House Publishers, Inc., 2016.
Identifiers: LCCN 2015047153| ISBN 9781496411839 (hc) | ISBN 9781496411846 (sc)
Subjects: LCSH: Prodan, Virginia. | Christian biography—Romania. | Church and
    state—Romania—History—20th century. | Persecution—Romania—History—
    20th century. | Romania—Politics and government—1944-1989. | Romania—
    Church history—20th century. | Ceaușescu, Nicolae.
Classification: LCC BR1725.P75 A3 2016 | DDC 274.98/082092—dc23 LC record
    available at http://lccn.loc.gov/2015047153

Printed in the United States of America

26   25   24   23   22
10   9   8   7   6   5

To Anca, Andreea, and Emanuel—my children

I should be dead.
Buried under an unmarked grave in Romania.

Obviously, I am not.
God had other plans.

VIRGINIA PRODAN

INTRODUCTION

Bucharest, Romania

1984

MIRUNA, MY LEGAL ASSISTANT, peeked into my office doorway. "A big man in the waiting room says he wants to discuss a case." She shrugged. "That's all he will tell me."

My desk lamp shed light over open books and files covering every inch of my large, cherry desk. I still had a mountain of work to do on a case to defend young Christians arrested for transporting Bibles. Noticing how late it was, I told her, "Go home. I'll see how I can help him."

I followed her to the waiting area where a broad, muscular man wearing a dark, expensively cut coat was seated. I motioned for him to follow me into my office.

At the doorway, I turned and noticed he towered over me. He ran his enormous hand over the silver doorplate reading, *Virginia Prodan, Attorney.* Then he closed the door behind him.

I met his eyes. They radiated an unsettling mix of pain, suffering, and cruelty, like the eyes of a bloodthirsty yet wounded lion.

A much-wounded man, I thought. *I hope I can help him.*

The slam of the waiting room door sounded, followed by the click of the outer door. My assistant was gone.

"Sit down!" The man pointed to one of the two chairs in front of my desk. His bushy brows formed an angry *V.* I swallowed a scream.

My blood chilled, and rapid-fire thumping pounded in my ears. I lowered myself into the chair. On the side table, my daughters, Anca and Andreea, smiled from framed photos.

The man sat in the other chair, pulled back his coat, and reached into a shoulder holster, withdrawing a gun.

"You have failed to heed the warnings you've been given," he said, pointing the gun toward me. My heart pounded against my chest like a courtroom gavel.

"I've come here to finish the matter once and for all." He flexed his fingers, and I heard the distinctive click of a trigger cocking into place.

"I am here to kill you."

CHAPTER 1

Techirghiol, Romania

1961

*You gain strength, courage, and confidence by every
experience in which you really stop to look fear in the face.
You are able to say to yourself, "I lived through this horror.
I can take the next thing that comes along."*

—ELEANOR ROOSEVELT

ON GOOD FRIDAY, it was customary for children to ask their
parents for forgiveness and to kiss their parents' hands—
a tradition that I always found awkward and strange. Then
we would go to the Romanian Orthodox Church so the
priest could offer us forgiveness. Sometimes I didn't even
know what I was asking forgiveness for. But it was the rule.
And in Techirghiol, you followed the rules or there were
consequences.

That day, I walked to the church with four neighbor girls.
As we entered the building, two tall men dressed in black
and sporting dark glasses blocked the doorway. One of them
opened a notebook. "Names! Ages!" he barked.

"*Securitate*," my friend whispered. *Communist government agents.*

My friends offered their names.

When it was my turn, I croaked, "Virginia Basta, age six."

One of the men stabbed his finger toward me. "You are now on the government's black list as *church people.*"

My friends rushed into the sanctuary. I followed and knelt on a small rug on the wooden floor. I bowed my head and prayed that God would keep me safe from those men. When I opened my eyes, my friends were gone. *They must have run out the side door.* I shivered. The church was cold, quiet, and desolate. The walls were draped with hand-painted icons of Jesus and Mary, and a serious-looking statue of Jesus seemed to watch me. *I will be brave! I won't run away because of those* Securitate *men.* I stayed on my knees for a long time, just to show those men I was not afraid. *Mother and Father always said we should be free in church.*

Two days later, during the Easter service, the priest sang in Latin outside the church. My stomach growled. We had fasted for a month. No meat, only vegetables. Easter was the only day my family attended church together. I wondered whether my parents were afraid of the *Securitate* men. I searched the crowd but didn't see their dark coats and sunglasses. Finally the priest snuffed out the candles, and we went home for an Easter feast of lamb, stuffing, and lots of cakes and cookies.

After Easter passed, the days grew warmer, but the *Securitate*'s hate-soaked words, *church people*, rang in my head for a long time. And though my family did not attend church on Sundays, sometimes on weekdays I'd slip through the doors and say a quick prayer on my way to school. Always, though, this came at great personal risk.

During the totalitarian regime of Nicolae Ceaușescu, the most brutal and repressive regime—even by Soviet bloc standards—Communist Romania was a land of lies. Religion was tolerated only to keep up outside appearances, and internal dissidence was not permitted. Ceaușescu's goal was to demolish the churches to make room for his palace—his earthly temple. Declaring himself a god, he decreed that he had brought about the "golden era," and every citizen was required to agree with him. If you did not, you would face the full wrath of Ceaușescu's secret police, the *Securitate*, one of the most ubiquitous and brutal secret police forces in the world. Simply put, Ceaușescu turned my native country into a prison land.

Not only were we not free to confront the lies of the despotic regime, but we lived in a constant state of anxiety and mistrust, as anyone could easily and often arbitrarily denounce a neighbor, classmate, or family member for making "antigovernment" statements. The best way to avoid punishment, I learned early on, was to remain silent and blend in.

Unfortunately, I did not blend in. And for that, I was punished.

My mother always had plenty of chores for me to do inside, while my older sister, Alina, my younger sister, Oana, and my younger brother, George, were allowed to play outside. In the beginning, I didn't pay any attention to this difference, nor to the fact that in the winter I had to wear a veil in public, and in the summer, a hat.

One afternoon while I was doing the dishes, I stood on my tiptoes to slide a plate into the cupboard, and through the open window, I could hear singing. "The sleeping bear is starving. We will feed him with milk or honey or coffee."

I leaned into the sink and tugged the curtain aside. Alina, Oana, George, and their friends were gathered in a circle playing *Ursual Doarme* (The Sleeping Bear). I loved that game.

My mother was asleep in the next room, and I knew that if I woke her to ask permission to play, she'd be as angry as a sleeping bear. But oh, how I wanted to join the fun!

I carefully cracked the back door open, then looked back toward the bedrooms. No sound. Quietly, I closed the door behind me and rushed to the outer edge of the circle in which Alina sat blindfolded. I bounced on my toes, hoping they'd let me play.

"See how her hair reflects the sun?" I turned toward the neighbor lady and her friend standing on the other side of the white wooden fence between our two yards.

"She's the only child in Techirghiol with red hair and freckles." She motioned toward me. "Come, Virginia."

I glanced at my sister—still blindfolded—and ran over to the fence.

The neighbor ran her fingers through my hair, then down my cheek. "Have you ever seen a child with so many freckles?" The other lady pulled a camera from her purse and snapped a picture. The neighbor pointed toward the other kids. "That's her sister in the center, her other sister over there, and her brother sitting at the edge of the circle."

Alina, Oana, and George all had black hair and olive skin. I had red hair and white skin with lots of freckles. I didn't know what to say in response to the neighbor's comment, so I said nothing.

"She's so tiny compared to them, even her younger brother."

"Virginia!" My mother stood in the doorway, arms folded. My mouth went dry as my mind raced to think of an excuse about why I'd left the house. I was in trouble. She motioned me inside.

After she spanked me, she went outside and collected fresh nuts and leaves, boiled them in a big pot, then rubbed the mucky black solution in my hair.

Later that evening, a ghostly looking girl with black hair, a white face, and red-rimmed eyes stared at me from the bathroom mirror. I picked up the cream she'd made me rub all over my face. Mother said it would make my freckles disappear. The lady on the jar didn't have one freckle on her face.

I was sorry I'd gone outside and made my mother mad. Now I'd have even more house chores for weeks to come. I looked into the mirror again at the new me. *Maybe if I looked normal like my sisters and brother, my family would love me more.* I twisted the cover tight on the cream, put it on the shelf, and ran to the kitchen for dinner.

"She still looks different." Alina scowled, crossing her arms.

My father's place sat empty. He worked in Constanta, four hours away, and was rarely at supper with the family, which was a shame for me. When he *was* home, Alina and my mother weren't nearly as mean.

My mother set a platter of fish and fries on the table. "Maybe we should find a family to adopt her," she said, looking at Alina.

My breath caught. I slid into the chair, blinking back tears. *What is wrong with me? Even with my red hair gone, my family doesn't want me.* I bit my lip. One adopted girl I knew in my class always cried during school and rubbed bruises on her arms. She'd fallen asleep in class once, and when I tapped her awake, she said she had been scrubbing floors all night.

"Please, Mother, don't send me away," I begged.

She placed a bowl of watermelon on the table. "A few families from the city are looking for a child to adopt. What do you think?" She looked from Alina to Oana to George. "Should we give her up for adoption?" She was serious.

"Nooooo!" I cried. Tears flooded my vision. I set my fork down and sobbed into the crook of my elbow. A jerk on my arm landed me on the floor. I stood and put my hands on my behind, then quickly removed them before the crack of the belt hit me.

"Go to bed!" Mother ordered, shoving me toward my bedroom.

As always, I did as I was told.

I climbed into my bed, rubbing my backside. *Maybe I*

could run away, I thought. *But what if those people looking for a child find me and take me away? They might beat me too.* I flipped my pillow over because it was damp with tears. I buried my face in the fabric to muffle my sobs. Crying would only bring Mother back in with her belt.

*

I set the black hair dye packet on the sink's ledge. For two years, Mother had been purchasing the store packets. She still occasionally threatened to put me up for adoption, but it never happened. I rinsed the sink, then shut off the water. The house was quiet. My family had left early that morning for summer vacation in Bucharest, where they would stay with my Aunt Cassandra. I hoped to meet Aunt Cassandra someday, but they never let me go with them, and questions or complaints would only earn me a sore bottom. Yet in my mind it didn't matter. Mother must have had *some* confidence in me to leave me in charge of the house. None of my friends, at age ten, were given that much responsibility. Besides, I had to work and earn money for the family.

Our town, Techirghiol, was famous for the supposed therapeutic effects of its lake and mud. An Ottoman commander visited in the 1850s, took several mud baths, and noticed amazing improvement on his ailing arm. By the time of my childhood, the waters brought a flood of summer visitors to town.

My family, like many families in Techirghiol, would make

extra money by renting out rooms in our home to visitors who came to take treatments. Most of these visitors came without reservations. Instead, when they arrived, they'd come to Dragalina Square, near the town's monument to war heroes, and seek connections with families that had rooms to rent.

Families in town would hire temporary workers to recruit these boarders. Usually the hired workers couldn't hold jobs elsewhere because of alcohol abuse, criminal records, or a history of violence. As temporary workers, they received cash after each job. My family used them too—until I turned seven years old.

Once I turned seven, I became the family's recruiter in the square. Over time, my work was extended to recruiting for other families in town too. I had to compete for business alongside the rough and ruthless adults. Some made inappropriate jokes; some smelled strongly of alcohol—even in the morning—or became drunk as soon as they received their first payment of the day; others were violent. Over the years, I watched many bloody fights break out on the square.

Why my family felt the need to take in boarders at all, I could not say. They didn't need the money. I can only surmise that they simply didn't want me around, and I knew enough not to ask questions or complain. They wouldn't have listened anyway, and my life would only have become harder.

One morning when I arrived at Dragalina Square, two of my competitors were having a fight, so I seized the opportunity. As the bus full of tourists pulled up, I quickly rushed up to the door, met the eyes of the first tourist to exit, and said, "Welcome to Techirghiol! My name is Virginia." And then, grabbing his suitcase, "If you need a room I can take you to my house. My parents have a lovely room that you could use. Would you like to follow me?"

"Yes," he responded, motioning to his wife behind him. "Thank you."

Just then, one of the men who had previously been fighting rushed over, pushed me aside, and blurted out, "Can I help you find a room, sir?"

"No, thank you. Virginia has already offered us a room."

"Well, I guess we can't compete with her charm," he said to his opponent, now standing behind me.

"*I'll* show her charm when she returns," the other man grumbled in response. Both men sneered at me angrily.

Walking away with my new clients, I tried to block out their angry words. *I'll deal with that later,* I thought. *Right now, I have to make sure this couple will take the room in my parents' house.*

Actually, I enjoyed getting to know these visitors and hearing their stories. Some of them almost became like friends. In fact, sometimes when they returned for future visits, they would stop by Dragalina Square to see me and ask how successful I had been that day.

Unfortunately, there were many days when I was not successful at all. Some days I stayed in Dragalina Square until ten at night hoping to find even one client. Eventually, hungry, sad, and exhausted, I would walk home, working on excuses for my lack of success that day—my failure, as my family would call it. As soon as I arrived home, I would try to go straight to bed, but always I was called to report.

"Today I started my day around five thirty in the morning at Dragalina Square," I would begin. "I took ten trips home with visitors, but none of them took a room. I also took them to the Popescu's, Amanar's, Enescu's, and Zaituc's houses, but none of them took their rooms either. And as you know, Popescu, Amanar, Enescu, and Zaituc all live far away from each other, so that took me some time also."

Mother looked neither pleased nor convinced.

"In between," I continued, "I stopped at the library and asked one of the workers, Maria, if she knew of any unhappy visitors who might be looking to change houses, and she assured me that she would send them directly to me if she heard anything."

Still nothing.

"Also, today some of the buses had mechanical problems, and a few of them never even arrived in town."

More silence.

I tried one last time.

"You know, I heard that many visitors prefer to stay in surrounding cities because of the strong, salty smell of Techirghiol Lake."

Somehow all the arguments that sounded so good on the way home suddenly sounded lame. I knew what was coming. Mother would bring out her belt, and after a severe beating and no dinner, I would cry myself to sleep—silently into my pillow, lest I disturb my siblings, who were exhausted from enjoying a day at the lake.

The morning after a failed day, I'd rise by five o'clock, grab a slice of bread and a piece of salami from the kitchen before anybody noticed me, and walk to the square hoping for a better day.

Walking down the quiet, deserted street, I would imagine the city belonged only to me. I would open my arms to greet the new day and the rising sun. The sun's warmth felt like the arms of a mother—not my mother perhaps, but what I always imagined a mother's warm embrace would feel like. My body and soul would be reenergized by mornings like those, and in my hardest hours, I would raise my head to the sky and imagine somebody was watching over me from above—somebody who loved me, red hair, pale skin, freckles, and all.

CHAPTER 2

Bad times have a scientific value.
These are occasions a good learner would not miss.

—RALPH WALDO EMERSON

I VIVIDLY REMEMBER the first time I was left alone and in charge of the house.

I was in first grade.

"Have a good trip," I said as my family departed. I acted courageous, but inside, my heart was aching.

Must be nice to see the world, I thought as tears ran down my face.

With the family gone from my view, I closed the gate, walked inside, locked the door behind me, and started putting all the dirty dishes in the sink. The house was quiet. Too quiet.

Then suddenly, someone hammered on the door. "I need

a cup of sugar, Elena! Why do you keep this door closed? Open the door!"

Terrified, I dropped the dish I was holding, ran to the opposite side of the house, jumped in my bed, and hid myself underneath the blanket.

The voice on the other side of the door grew louder, as did the hammering. "I need some sugar. I don't want to walk to the store. Elena, open the door!"

I thought the door would come down. I didn't move underneath my blanket.

Finally the house became quiet again. I pulled the blanket off my face and looked out the window facing me. All I could see were the branches of the tree out back swaying gently in the breeze. I started to imagine friendly faces in the branches—almost as though someone were watching over me. Strangely, I felt protected. From that day forward, imagining friendly faces in the branches became a game to help combat my fear and loneliness.

I also discovered another way to escape and make friends—through books.

One afternoon while the family was in Bucharest visiting Aunt Cassandra, I grabbed a book and stepped outside. Setting Brontë's *Jane Eyre* down on the ground, I climbed onto a tree swing, pushed off, pumped hard, then tucked my legs underneath me. I leaned back and followed the path of an airplane cutting a line through the sky. *Someday,* I thought, *I'll fly away from here and travel the world.* I closed my eyes. As I slowed, I imagined the swing was my mother, rocking me, telling me everything would be okay.

I looked out beyond my front gate and thought, *I could run away and be miles from here before they returned.* It wasn't the first time I'd fantasized about leaving. Many nights lying in bed, I'd plan my escape, but I would usually fall asleep before I formed a solid plan. I stared back up into the sky. *But then again,* I mused, *where would I go?*

I was trapped.

The breeze blew a leaf across my novel, reminding me that I wasn't alone. My friends were in my books, and with them I could travel to wonderful places on my own vacations. I traveled to Spain with Ernest Hemingway in the pages of *For Whom the Bell Tolls* and witnessed the tale of a young American who fought and died there. I was transported to the American Civil War with Harriet Beecher Stowe, the little lady who—according to President Lincoln—started that big war. Her book, *Uncle Tom's Cabin,* showed me the merciless reality of slavery. It also showed me how love can heal. *Shogun* introduced me to the Japanese culture and educated me on the Japanese art of flower arranging called ikebana.

As each fictional character became my new friend, I took courage. I recognized that "the future belongs to those who believe in the beauty of their dreams," as Eleanor Roosevelt said.

I rose from the swing and picked up *Jane Eyre.* I'd read it twice already. I understood Jane. Her adopted parents detested her quiet but passionate character. They also hated how she looked. Yet she was hardworking, honest, patient, and passionate. Just like me.

One day my life would be wonderful, like the lives of the characters in my books. I needed only to be patient, like Jane.

My musings were quickly interrupted by a voice I didn't recognize.

"I'll tell your past and predict your future for food, clothes, or money."

I raised my head from my book. Gypsies! The ladies in layers of long skirts carrying babies on their hips chattered quickly about how they could help me. Their big gold earrings wagged as they nodded their heads.

"What do you know about my past?" I asked. Gypsies were known to steal kids, but maybe they only meant to help me. I gingerly approached them.

"Go! Leave that girl alone!" A neighbor lady, coming home from the market with her daughter, quickly waved them away. Then she shook her finger at me. "You should be happy in your present. Nothing good will come from looking at your past."

The Gypsies shuffled on, jewelry jingling as they left. As the neighbor walked into the house, I heard her daughter say, "She doesn't need a Gypsy to tell her she's not a member of *that* family."

I gripped the rope on the swing. Heat rushed to my head. My heart pounded. I shook my head and hugged the book under my arm. Would I be surprised to find out I wasn't a member of my family? Probably not. I didn't look like any of them, and they didn't treat me as though I belonged. I only wished I knew the truth about where I *did* come from.

That night, I lay in bed, thinking about what the neighbor and her daughter had unknowingly revealed to me. A growl erupted from my stomach. There were only stale crackers in the cupboard. *A real family would not have left me for weeks with little food and no money.*

A thud on the side of the house made me bolt upright in my bed. *Was someone coming to kidnap me? The Gypsies? Were they back?* I peeked out my window. Branches swayed and tapped the house. Not Gypsies. Maybe a limb had fallen against the house. I studied the shadows of the nearby trees. Those trees were strong, like a fortress. *I need to be strong too.* I sighed and slunk under my covers. I needed sleep and strength for work tomorrow.

*

Even though I knew them only through the stories I read, I knew a lot more about my imaginary friends than I did about my parents, Stephen and Elena.

I knew that Stephen was much older than Elena and that sometimes he acted more like a grandfather than a father. He loved our dog, Azorel, so much that upon coming home from work, he would go to see Azorel first and *then* come to see us. He exercised his parental authority only if Elena was upset with us—otherwise she was the strong, powerful disciplinarian, especially toward me. Sometimes even an innocent question could result in belt whippings, spankings, or being sent to bed without food. She made it clear to me that I was there to serve her and to keep quiet, and nothing else.

Stephen seldom punished me; on the other hand, I seldom got his attention or got to spend time with him. The only times I felt he acted as a father to me were the few times he received promotions and would come home tipsy. Then he was funny, and he played with me, gave me gifts, and made me feel like I was his daughter.

For example, one afternoon I was cleaning the kitchen floor when I heard the door open so wide that it slammed into the wall behind it. Stephen appeared outside the door, hardly keeping his balance. He hesitated for a few seconds, trying to take his next step, and his arms were full of gifts.

"Dad is home!" Oana screamed behind me, and she and George came running to the door.

Holding on to the door for balance, Stephen handed out his gifts. "A new baby doll for Alina. A stroller for your doll, Oana; a fire truck for you, George."

And then to me, he said, "Bring me the baby doll I gave you last year, Virginia!"

So I ran and brought him the doll.

"Here is a new dress for your doll." Stephen knelt down beside me and helped me dress my doll. His breath almost made me dizzy. With his big fingers he managed to close the baby doll's dress. He tickled me as he returned the doll to me.

"Do you like it?" he asked. "Arnel, my coworker, gave

it to me for you. It is a dress from East Germany, from his relatives." I looked up and saw an ocean of love in his eyes.

Then Elena came in. "Did you get drunk with your friends again?" she boomed. "Get up and take a shower! You are disgusting. Stop being silly, playing with dolls like a child!"

Then she grabbed me by the back of the neck. "Put that doll away," she bellowed. "Finish the floor and set the dinner table!"

I never met Stephen's parents, but I had heard that his mother wanted him to be a tailor, so she bought him a sewing machine, which stayed in our house forever. He did not want to be a tailor, so to escape the training and without his mother's permission, he joined the army and served in World War II. He rarely talked about his experiences there, but one night the rest of the family dozed off as we were watching a war movie on TV, and Stephen and I were the only ones left awake. As the soldiers on the screen dodged an explosion, sending blizzards of dirt into the air, he started to sob.

"What's wrong?" I asked. "If you don't like this movie, we don't have to watch it."

As I gently rubbed his back, he began to speak in a hushed tone.

"I was in the battlefield, hidden with my battalion in a trench, when suddenly the world changed into darkness. A bomb exploded not far from us. Death buried me. My nose and throat were full of mud. I panicked. I couldn't move. I could see my entire life playing out in front of me."

He stifled a sob. "Then came another explosion, and I found myself flying in the air. I landed hard on my back. Oh! It hurt so badly. Nevertheless, I felt free and alive. I could see and feel again. I looked around, but no one else was there with me." He buried his face in his hands, and his shoulders began to shake with the memory of watching his friends die.

That night I saw something sensitive and special in his soul. He had always been the calmer of the two. Perhaps his time on the battlefield had taught him to cope with stress and disappointment better than most.

Elena, on the other hand, was very moody and quick to anger, and she easily found fault with others. According to her, something was wrong all the time. During every New Year's party, while everybody else was happily celebrating, she cried for the lost year. Sometimes it seemed as though she cried constantly. The only time I did not see her crying was during the birthday parties she planned for Alina, Oana, and George. She would cook special meals, decorate the house, buy gifts, and invite all the children from the neighborhood to celebrate—for Alina, Oana, and George. Not once in eighteen years did she ever have a party or bake a cake for my birthday. She said that by January second, everybody was too tired from the holidays to celebrate anything else—least of all me. I always felt guilty for being born on that day. Most days, I felt guilty for being born at all.

One afternoon as I was washing the dishes, Elena called out, "Everyone come to the dining room." Alina, Oana, and George all came running from their rooms. I kept working.

"Virginia, do I have to come and get you?"

What? I marveled. Typically, the word *everyone* did not apply to me. I turned to look at her, and she released an exasperated sigh and waved me over.

Alina, Oana, and George all took seats at the table. I remained standing, still clutching a dishcloth.

"Today I visited my friend Mahala, the Gypsy fortune-teller," she began. "She told me that Virginia—yes, you—" she said, pointing at me, "will acquire an indescribable inheritance." She stopped and looked directly at me. I could feel my heart beating faster.

"Mahala said that Virginia will live a long and happy life in a *rich city*," she said, slowly emphasizing those final two words.

My mind raced. *What is she talking about? What shall I say to her? How can I get out of this unpunished?* The tension was quickly broken by Alina.

"Why Virginia? Why her? Who is she?" she whined.

"What about me?" Oana and George asked simultaneously.

"Nothing." Elena shook her head, still staring at me.

"We need to have a serious family talk, Mom!" Alina announced, clearly annoyed.

"Go back to your chores, Virginia." Elena brushed me away with her hand, but her eyes never left mine.

Confused and frightened, I retreated to the kitchen.

Moments later, Alina appeared in the doorway. "We are going out to dinner and to the movies with Mom and Dad," she stated, still visibly annoyed. "When we return, make sure everything on your chores list is done."

"Yes, of course," I immediately responded. *At least for now I am safe,* I thought. *But what did the fortune-teller mean? Whom would I possibly receive a great inheritance from? Certainly not Stephen and Elena.* And while Techirghiol was known for many things, great wealth was not one of them. *But where else would I go? And how would I get there?*

The questions continued to play in my mind late into the evening and well into the coming weeks. Yet another reminder that I was different—that I didn't belong.

CHAPTER 3

*The bravest sight in the world
is to see a great man struggling
against adversity.*

—SENECA

SUMMER'S END WAS marked by three events that I looked
forward to each year: the end of my work on the square, the
start of school, and the grape harvest.

Around the west part of our house sprawled row upon
row of vines heavy with black and white grapes, and every
summer, my father's extended family—cousins, aunts, and
uncles—made the trip from Constanta for the harvest, and
a week of fun began.

I loved collecting grapes from the vineyard, putting them
into the special machine, and seeing them changed into a
sweet liquid. From the white and black grapes, my family
made sugary grape juice for the kids and wine for the adults.

The summer that I was seven years old, my family and relatives retired to the front porch after dinner to enjoy their last evening in Techirghiol. Around midnight, startling screams cut the still night.

"That's Anna," Mother said. "Our neighbor's granddaughter."

The screams continued from next door. "Nooooo! Don't kill them."

Kill whom? I glanced toward my parents. Often our neighbor girl, Anna, screamed in the night, but I didn't know why. She lived with her grandparents next door, but I didn't see her often, and I was warned not to talk to her. Each scream cinched my heart and seared all the way through to my gut. I wrapped my arms around myself. I looked from my parents to my relatives, hoping for answers.

Mother frowned and waved her hand like she was swatting away a mosquito. "Let's go inside. That home is supervised." She nodded toward the house, and everyone rose.

Seated in the family room, my relatives shook their heads, but no one spoke or moved to help. One of my uncles mumbled something. My aunt, an attorney, put her finger to her lips. "Don't speak. Too dangerous."

So they conversed in whispers. I heard bits and pieces about how just a few months ago, the *Securitate* had taken my aunt's coworker to an unknown location for a month because he was accused of missing participation in a Party parade. When the coworker returned home, his health was visibly deteriorated, and he was unable to work or provide for his family.

My nails dug into my hands. *What is everybody so afraid of? Why do they speak in whispers? Why doesn't anyone help Anna?* Everyone looked toward the relatives who were lawyers. Did they know something? Two lawyers nodded, passing knowing looks. One said a fellow attorney who had expressed his concern about the new price on meat disappeared between the courthouse and his home, never to be found. His children would not be allowed to apply to law school. Instead, the *Securitate* required them to take construction jobs.

Many of the adults, it seemed, carried secrets. I bit my lip to hold in the questions that ran through my mind. *Does this have anything to do with the men who guarded the church years ago and called my friends and me "church people"? Were Anna's parents church people? What happened to them? Why does she scream so often in the night?*

"Liars!" The voice came from the back bedroom where Uncle Carol was resting.

My mother rubbed her temples. Uncle Antony, Uncle Carol's son, groaned.

I hustled to the back bedroom. My job was to take care of Uncle Carol, bringing him food and making sure he was okay. Everyone treated him like a sick person, but he seemed normal to me.

"Criminals!"

"Uncle Carol, what's wrong?"

Before Uncle Carol could answer, Uncle Antony stepped into the room, his face as red as the juice from the grapes we'd pressed earlier. "Do you want the *Securitate* to put you in the hospital again?"

"At least there I will be free to speak my mind."

Uncle Antony knelt at his father's feet and grasped his hands. "What about me? I don't want to be confined in the psychiatric hospital. You know they will take me this time if you don't stop talking."

Uncle Carol held his son's gaze then lowered his head. "I will be quiet for you, but I will not be free." I saw many emotions pass between them—cooperation and resistance mixed with love and hate. *Why?*

Uncle Antony returned to the family room. I knelt beside Uncle Carol. "Do you want a drink of water?" He nodded, then another scream from next door reached our ears. He pressed his hand against his chest.

I ran to the kitchen and poured a glass of water. Passing the family room, I stopped in the doorway at the mention of Anna's name. Today was her birthday, my mother was saying. "She had her own wing in the family mansion across town long before her birth." I had passed that home—a massive white stone mansion overlooking the lake—many times in my travels across Techirghiol. Although it was now a kind of hotel, I could not bring my clients of ordinary people from Dragalina Square to its doors. It was reserved for Communist Party leaders on vacation.

From the conversation, I heard about Anna growing up with nannies, servants, a personal tutor, and a driver. I heard about her travels with her parents all over the world, until her tenth birthday. At that point in the story, my mother glanced up and frowned upon seeing me. "Virginia, sleep on the sofa in the room with Uncle Carol. Take care of him."

I returned to the bedroom. Uncle Carol appeared to be asleep. I set the water on the table by his bed and tucked myself into the sofa bed on the other side of the room.

"Virginia, do you want to know the truth about Anna?"

"Yes!" I tossed off my covers, switched on the lamp, and rushed to his side.

Uncle Carol stared at the ceiling. "I will tell you, if you promise never to tell anyone you heard it from me."

"I promise."

"I was there at her house for her tenth birthday. She wore a long pink dress with many white roses down the front. Her small white shoes matched the roses. She was simply radiant." Uncle Carol focused on the ceiling, but his mind was clearly at Anna's party. "Her parents were so proud. They'd just returned from her first trip to Paris. What a dinner they had that night."

I wanted to ask him so many questions but was afraid to interrupt.

"Afterward, Anna opened gifts, then began her piano recital. The chandeliers shed a bright light over the big black piano. Anna arranged her music, looked to her piano teacher, nodded, and began to play."

Uncle Carol sat up. "The music stopped." His cheerful voice grew sad. "The giant ballroom doors burst open. Violent noises and angry shouts! The Romanian Communist armed military group pointed guns around the room. Their leader, a tall young officer, ordered Anna's parents, John and Maria, to stand and follow him." Uncle Carol put his hands over his face and sobbed.

I sat beside him and hugged him.

"Anna was scared because she'd never heard anyone give orders to her parents before. Her tutor touched her shoulder to comfort her, but she hurried to her parents, who were on their knees and had been handcuffed and brutally beaten by the two armed officers. Her older brother, Jim, was also handcuffed. The armed military officers dragged them away with much commotion but no explanation. When Anna asked why, a young officer slapped and shoved her, causing her to fall backward. He said, 'This is how we treat our enemies. If you are not with us, you are against us.' Then he claimed the house belonged to the government."

Uncle Carol rocked back and forth on the edge of the bed. "I was silent when they handcuffed and struck her parents. Too afraid to talk or move. I can never forgive myself." Tears streamed down his face. "I was among the first to run when Anna's parents and brother were dragged away. I returned later for Anna, but it was too late. Government officials had taken her to one orphanage after another, changing her name with each move so that it was impossible to trace her. The young Communist officer, Boris, took control of Anna's parents' mansion and established his residence there. I grew more afraid, thinking I would suffer the same fate as her parents. I took a long business trip to London. When I returned to my work at the bank, armed guards had threatened my trusted partner, Martin, and 'persuaded' him to turn over all of Anna's parents' bank accounts, safes, and valuables."

Uncle Carol turned to me. "What was I supposed to do?"

How could I answer?

"Boris returned to check on me. He even promised that if I collaborated with him, he would help me find Anna and her relatives. I felt so guilty, and I wanted to find Anna and her relatives, so I accepted his proposition."

I glanced toward the door, worried his raised voice would bring in Uncle Antony again. Elena would punish me for not keeping my uncle calm.

"Liars, criminals!"

"Shh! You told Uncle Antony you wouldn't shout."

He nodded and lowered his voice. I held my breath, wondering why he was telling me this story, yet hoping he'd continue.

"One day, as I confronted Boris about his lies, he picked up the phone, and soon his guards arrived and put me in the psychiatric hospital. That was the only place where I was free to speak my mind—until nurses drugged me. Many were not afraid to speak the truth there." He shrugged. "But too sad there."

"How did Anna come to live next door to us?"

"At each orphanage Anna was sent to, she spent several days answering questions from the police and other government authorities regarding her parents and other relatives and the type of safes, jewelry, and guns her parents had. Finally they must have gotten all the information they wanted, so Anna was sent to her grandparents' home, next door to your house."

"Why doesn't anyone help her now?"

"Because they know the truth."

"I want to know the truth."

He patted my hands. "Go to sleep."

I rose, and he tugged my hand. "You don't think I am sick, do you, Virginia?"

"No," I responded. "I think you are very healthy."

He smiled. "I don't remember the last time my son said that to me."

I hugged him good night. He brushed my hair with his hands, looked into my eyes, and smiled. Then he reclined and closed his eyes. After a few minutes, a soft snore filled the room.

I tucked myself back in my bed. That night I knew in my heart that I wanted to become a lawyer. I wanted to find out the truth—what had happened to Anna's parents and why everyone was still afraid to help her. I also wanted to find out the truth about myself and who I really was. Of all our relatives, only Uncle Carol treated me like family, and everyone considered him a sick, crazy old man. *Were my real parents taken away like Anna's?* I wondered. At least that would explain why I didn't look like anyone else in my family—and why I was treated so differently from everyone else. Maybe Stephen and Elena were forced to take me in by the *Securitate*. Or maybe I was just crazy, like they said Uncle Carol was.

For years those familiar screams—Anna pleading for her parents' lives—carried into my bedroom. Her body grew, but mentally she remained a ten-year-old.

People ridiculed her, but after hearing her story, I understood that she had to make her own world in order to survive. Fear, death, and suspicion looked at me through the bars of the iron fence that divided our property; they taught me about what Communism could do to a person. Sometimes I'd watch Anna, or wave, or offer a friendly word, regardless of the warnings. Like going to church, being friends with Anna would have meant I was an enemy of the government.

Uncle Carol was put into psychiatric hospitals twice more. After the second time, he was released to his son's home. He remained inside his room, refusing to eat and dying with the wish upon his lips that he would have spoken up for Anna. Although others knew him as the "crazy relative," I believed him to be brave.

*

By the time I started my freshman year of high school, Alina had graduated from the University of Bucharest Law School. Soon after this, she married an engineer, moved with him to his hometown, and started to work there as a government attorney.

When my family returned from Alina's wedding, Stephen and Elena decided I would remain in Techirghiol to take care of them once I finished high school.

When I heard this pronouncement, my stomach turned and my brain froze. While this decision that held my future captive frightened me, it made me all the more determined to go to law school. I suppose none of us know how high we can jump until a skyscraper obstructs our way, how fast we can run until a lion chases us, the value of our freedom until confinement restricts our movements, or how precious hope is until someone shatters our dreams.

Even though I never accepted that future as my own, I decided to keep my mouth shut, avoid conflict with the family, do all my chores, and unwaveringly pursue every opportunity to study for my baccalaureate and law school exams.

Methodically, as soon as I finished all my chores, I locked myself in an unused room in the house and studied until past midnight. When the time came, I filed for approval of my political file to pave my way into law school.

Under the Communist system, students had to pass two levels of admission to get into law school. In the first level, my political file had to pass inspection. An approved file verified three things:

1. The applicant and his or her parents had never expressed a critical attitude toward Communism.
2. The applicant's parents had never been questioned or arrested by the Communist government.
3. The applicant's parents were not Christians.

The Communist regime selected loyal leaders via this process. The graduates of law schools became the attorney general, minister of justice, ambassadors, judges, or attorneys to advance and protect the Communist agenda and fight against those people called "dissidents."

For a few months, everything worked well, but soon Elena considered my study time a waste of electricity. So instead I got up every morning by five o'clock, before anybody else awoke, and studied outside. Bundled up with warm clothes and sometimes even gloves, holding my book and outlines, pacing in front of my house to keep warm, I meticulously and desperately studied; even the semidark, cold, snowy months of winter and the rainy mornings of spring did not deter me.

Parents of my schoolmates and friends would pass by, see me hard at work, and admire my study habits. Unknowingly, I became a symbol of a hard-working student within the community. Little did they know the reasons behind my study habits.

My final year in high school found me working hard with my teachers to prepare for law school entrance exams. Since I was the only one in my class aiming for law school, my teacher, Sherban, had spent many hours with me throughout my high school years making sure that I would be fully prepared for the exam. Sometimes he would surprise me by asking me to do an extemporaneous oral presentation on a subject he chose. To my amazement and joy, I could always answer the questions, give thoughtful presentations, and make good grades. That boosted my confidence and energized me to work harder. He also encouraged me to compete in academic decathlons. Under his supervision, I studied hard and won many of the competitions. Every time I won, I gained self-confidence. I was seventeen and a half, and I believed I could conquer the world. It was a great feeling. I knew everything—*except* how to exercise freedom of choice.

All my life, either Elena or my teachers had told me what to do, and I had to follow their directions to a T. I always had to stay within the boundaries of my chores or homework to avoid punishment. I couldn't choose the time or manner in which to do them. I had never had any occasion to decide for myself.

Once, Sherban gave an exam unlike any we had ever experienced. Instead of assigning us a subject to write about or listing questions to answer, he asked us to choose our own subject from the class material. I found myself staring at a blank notebook, unsure of what to do. I knew the class material better than anybody, but that did not help. I had to *choose*, and I was not used to choosing. I rocked from astonishment to wonder to perplexity to fear. *Why can't he just tell us what to write about?* It seemed as though an eternity had passed before I finally began writing.

I chose to write about my hero, Mircea cel Batran, later known as Mircea the Great. Mircea ruled Wallachia, an important state of Romania, from 1386 to 1418. He was a wise and great military leader, and he was a fair ruler to all. Many Romanians consider Mircea to be the bravest and ablest of the Christian princes. Not only did he bring great stability to both the state and the country, he was also a strong supporter of the Church, building many beautiful churches in Romania, including one of my favorites, the Cozia Monastery.

I don't know what inspired me to write about Mircea that day. But there was one thing I did know for certain. I would have given anything to live under Mircea's reign. *What would it feel like,* I wondered, *to live in a society where people told and valued the truth? What would it be like to experience true freedom?* As I reviewed my essay, I marveled at how much Mircea had accomplished—and my heart sank at the sobering realization of how much the people of Romania had lost under Communist rule.

I could feel my resolve strengthening. I *would* become an attorney. And when I did, I would dedicate myself to the constant pursuit of truth and freedom—just like Mircea the Great.

CHAPTER 4

Never give up, for that is just the
place and time that the tide will turn.

—HARRIET BEECHER STOWE

ON MAY 12 OF my senior year of high school, I passed the
baccalaureate exam. Two days later, I received approval of my
political file and the invitation to take the second step toward
law school: admission exams. To my surprise, Elena agreed
without any arguments that I could take the exams. In fact,
she decided that during the three weeks of my exams, I could
stay with my Aunt Cassandra.

Flying on the wings of my dreams, equipped with all my
knowledge, my books, and the clothes on my back, I boarded
the train to Bucharest. At eighteen, I was traveling alone for
the first time. It was a three-hour adventure. The train, the
passengers, and each place we passed mesmerized me. Several

passengers in my compartment played cards, while others exchanged stories about cities we passed or about themselves. I had only one story: I was going to take and pass the law school exam! I did not have a plan B because I would not accept one.

I enjoyed seeing every station where the train stopped, but as soon as I arrived at my final destination, I noticed that the Bucharest train station was a distinctive, monumental, and remarkably modern station. Between the two World Wars, Bucharest was called the "Paris of the East," and the station was a testament to how modern and developed Romania had been—before World War II and Communist rule had wreaked destruction on it. Throngs of people entered and exited—such crowds as I'd never seen.

In a blink of an eye, everybody from my train compartment disappeared. I grabbed my bag of books and slowly walked to the visitors' center to find Aunt Cassandra. Over the crowd, I heard a loud and joyful voice screaming my name.

Before I even saw her face, Aunt Cassandra had enveloped me in a giant hug.

"You are finally here!" she exclaimed, hugging me even tighter. I was speechless. Nobody in my family had ever been this excited to see me. Nor had they ever shown me this much affection.

When Aunt Cassandra finally released her grasp so that I could see her, my breath caught in my chest. Cassandra was a petite woman with short red hair that framed a pale but radiant face dotted with a few freckles. *Remarkable,* I thought. *She looks just like me.*

"Oh! Turn around. I want to see you." Cassandra beamed. "Green is such a good color for you. And just look at you. You are as tall as I am!"

As Cassandra prattled on excitedly about my clothing and my trip, I stood speechless. All these years, I had never been allowed to visit Aunt Cassandra with the rest of the family. And now I knew why. Finally, there was a family member I actually resembled! A deep sense of relief washed over me like a flood, followed by the sobering realization—*No wonder Elena wanted to keep this a secret. It would have made me happy. It would have made me feel as though I might actually belong.*

We took a taxi from the train station to Cassandra's house. I had heard Elena and my siblings talk about Bucharest before, but nothing could have prepared me for this. The city looked far bigger and more exciting than I was told to expect. Broad streets, old stone buildings surrounded by tall trees and vivid flowers, and superb architecture combined to form my first impression of the city. When we passed the elegant white building that housed the University of Bucharest Law School, my heart beat so fast I could hear it echo in my ears.

Cassandra's house was very tidy and smelled of fresh-cut roses. When she led me to the room that would belong to me during my stay, I was stunned. It was big and bright with a full-size bed, two stands with lamps, a small desk, and two cross-stitch samplers on the wall—one with my name on it and the other with my birthday. Everything looked new and joyful. It was nothing like my room in Techirghiol, which was tiny, dark, and dingy. It was as though I had entered a whole new world, and for the first time in my life, I felt special.

After I got settled, Cassandra and I had lunch. As I stuffed myself with bread and fruit and cheese, Cassandra simply sat back and stared at me—in amazement, it seemed.

"I just cannot believe you are actually here," she said, her eyes glistening with tears. I wasn't sure how to react. Nobody had ever been this happy to have me around before.

Later we walked to the stores, and it was my turn to stare in amazement. I had never seen such beautiful clothing before. The variety of colors and styles was overwhelming.

"This one is beautiful," Cassandra remarked, holding up a gorgeous red dress. "Do you like it?"

I nodded, voiceless as Cassandra continued pulling different dresses off the rack. "Look at this one," she continued, holding up a simple green dress. "What do you think about this color? It would look beautiful with your coloring."

I was almost giddy with excitement. Nobody had ever referred to my coloring as beautiful before. But then, until now I had never known anybody *with* my coloring before. As I watched Cassandra continue to comb through rack after rack of dresses, I couldn't get over how different she was from everyone else in my family. Everything about her set her apart. She was bright, funny, joyful, energetic—everything Elena was not.

"You choose which ones you like, Virginia—after all, you

are going to be the one to wear them," she proclaimed, holding out several dresses at once.

Wear them? The thought paralyzed me. *She's buying these dresses for* me?

"There is the dressing room," she said, nodding toward the left and handing me the dresses. "Try them on and see how they look."

Weighed down with fabric, ribbons, and lace, I stumbled toward the dressing room. As soon as the door closed behind me, tears started cascading down my cheeks. I draped the dresses over the back of the chair, pressed my back up against the wall, and slowly slid to the floor, my head swimming.

My own room. A delicious lunch. Shopping. So much kindness. It was almost too much to bear.

"Here are a few pairs of shoes for you to try on with your dresses," Cassandra said, passing two simple yet beautiful pairs of low heels over the top of the door.

"Thank you," I managed, standing up to take the shoes. Wiping my cheeks, I set the shoes down and picked up the green dress Cassandra had said would look good with my coloring. I held it in front of me and looked in the mirror. All my life, I had worn Alina's hand-me-downs. By the time they came to me, they were usually quite worn, almost threadbare in spots. But this fabric was weighty and crisp, and it smelled so . . . *new.* I slipped the dress on over my head, almost afraid to let it touch my skin. It looked beautiful.

"Have you chosen something?" Cassandra called from outside the door. "Let me see."

I gingerly stepped outside.

"Oh, Virginia! You look so beautiful!" Cassandra beamed, her eyes filling with tears.

There was that word again. In spite of every instinct, I felt my lips curl into a smile.

"Really?" I asked, my face reddening.

"Yes," Cassandra replied, stepping forward to adjust one of my sleeves. "Beautiful."

Aunt Cassandra bought me two dresses that day—a red one with an intricate white lace design and, of course, the green one that had looked so perfect against my pale complexion. She also bought me two pairs of shoes. They were the first completely new outfits I had ever owned, the first things that had truly belonged only to me. That night, I left both outfits outside of my wardrobe so I could stare at them as I fell asleep and so they would be the first things I would see in the morning.

*

The next morning, I began reviewing for my law school exams. It felt good to study inside the house for a change. Throughout the day, Cassandra brought me all kinds of goodies to snack on. The house was silent, and I was able to study for hours without interruption or chores. I noticed that Cassandra even stopped listening to the radio while I worked, instead busying herself with needlework so as not to disturb me.

One day she showed me one of her finished projects, and

I cried. When she asked me why, I replied, "Because you have finished your work, and I have not yet finished my exams."

Her sweet response shocked me. "Well, I will just have to start a larger needlework so you can finish before me."

In addition to being incredibly kind, she was also full of surprises. One day, for example, she announced that she had made an appointment for us to have a professional picture taken.

"But why?" I asked.

"So that I will always have a reminder of you," she said, hugging me tight. "I've waited so long to see you. I don't ever want to forget this time together."

As she gently caressed my back, my mind wandered to Elena, and I found myself wondering if she was missing me at all.

Probably not, I thought. Except, perhaps, after meals, when someone else would have to do the dishes.

When we got to the photographer's studio, I couldn't help but overhear several people comment on how much Cassandra and I resembled each other. I could have sworn I heard the words *mother* and *daughter* mumbled in hushed tones. Even the photographer made a comment to that effect. "The family resemblance is amazing," he said, peering through his lens. "You and your daughter have the same fair skin, hair, and eyes."

I looked at Cassandra, waiting for her to correct him, but she simply stood there smiling and grasping my hand, neither confirming nor contradicting his assumption.

*

Every evening, I would take a study break, and Cassandra and I would take long walks in the Cişmigiu Park and talk about different law schools. There were only three in all of Romania: Bucharest, Cluj, and Iasi. I knew Bucharest was the largest and the best, offering only one hundred places each year with more than thirty candidates competing for each open spot. But Cassandra was familiar with every detail of the exams' procedures.

Before I could take the exams, I had to register with the law school and present several documents—my high school diploma, a record of my grades, medical documents, letters of recommendation from local Communist leaders, documents confirming that my parents had never been arrested, and many more. Knowing that the line to the registrar's office would be long each day of the two to three weeks before the entrance exams, Cassandra offered to stand in line and submit my paperwork for me so that I could spend that time studying. She also committed to praying and fasting for me for two weeks, a sacrifice made all the greater given Cassandra's love of food and cooking. Her care, generosity, and love amazed me. *She is* nothing *like the rest of the family,* I realized.

The morning of my first day of exams came sooner than I would have liked. The sky was clear blue. The birds were singing. And I was nervous. Unable to eat and pacing in my room, I saw a dove on the balcony and wishfully considered it a sign of God's favor.

Putting on a beautiful navy dress with a white collar that Cassandra had bought especially for this occasion, I hurried to get to the law school building, only to be met by a sea of candidates already waiting in the courtyard. After what seemed like an eternity, we all filed into the amphitheater where we were to take our exams. The room was packed. As the instructors began passing out the exam booklets, I gazed around the room to size up my competition. *So many people all wanting to become attorneys,* I thought. I felt both encouraged and disheartened. Encouraged because there were so many others who, like me, valued and wanted to spend their lives searching for the truth. And yet, *so many people . . .* I took a deep breath and steeled myself for the exam.

That day's series of exams comprised three essay questions, which I would have four hours to answer. I scanned the questions.

1. Compare and contrast Fascist Italy/Nazi Germany to the Romanian Revolution.
2. Describe the new Civic Rights after the Romanian Communist Revolution.
3. Discuss the role of women in Romania.

This was going to be a long day.

Throughout the morning, I didn't pay attention to anyone or anything around me. I focused entirely on the exam. The boy who sat behind me, however, was a tad distracted. When we first sat down, he introduced himself as Radu, and throughout the exam, he kept clearing his throat and on several occasions pretended to sneeze so I would turn and offer a "Bless you," after which he would always smile, wink, and say, "Thank you."

On the second day of written exams, he finished early and went out to the courtyard to strike up a conversation with Cassandra, who was waiting to walk me home.

"Your daughter is still writing," he told her. "She is working very hard on her exam."

"Oh, good," she responded. "I am glad to hear that. She was pretty nervous this morning."

"You have a beautiful girl, ma'am," he said, smiling at Cassandra. "May I call her at home?"

"Of course you may," she responded, giving him her number. I saw them talking, but by the time I reached Cassandra, Radu had gone.

"What was that all about?" I asked Cassandra.

"Oh, that nice boy was just telling me how hard you have been working on your exams," she said. And then, smiling, "He thinks you're very beautiful."

"But how did he know who you were?" I pressed her.

"Oh, I don't know. We do look a lot alike. Perhaps he just guessed. How did your exams go?"

"Fine," I said, distracted. I quickly scanned the courtyard to see if I could see him.

"Do you think you did well enough to make it through to the oral exams?" she asked.

I turned my gaze back to her. "I hope so. I don't think

Elena would let me come back to try again next year."
Actually, I knew she wouldn't. It was a miracle she'd let me
come now.

"Come on," Cassandra said, draping her arm over my
shoulder. "You must be starving. I've got a huge dinner waiting for you at home." And then she winked at me. "And my
fast is officially over."

That evening, shortly after we finished dinner, the phone
rang.

"It's for you," Cassandra said, handing me the receiver.

Since neither Elena nor Stephen had called since I left
Techirghiol, and I didn't know anyone else in Bucharest,
I had a pretty good idea who was on the other end.

"Hello?" I said. As expected, it was Radu.

"I'm fine, thanks. How did you find out my aunt's phone
number? Oh, she did." I shot a glance over at Cassandra,
who smiled coyly and winked. "No, she's not my mother.
She's my aunt. Yes, I know. We look a lot alike. Thank you.
Perhaps. Maybe after the exams are all finished. Yes. You
too. Good-bye."

"Well, a good day with your exams, and now this."
Cassandra beamed. "I would say Bucharest agrees with you."

Maybe so, I thought. But it would still be several days
before I would find out if I was accepted into the law school.
The thought of not finding my name on that list and having
to return home to Techirghiol a failure was almost more than
I could bear.

I simply can't go home, I thought. *Not now. Everything here is so wonderful, and I love Aunt Cassandra so much. I have to make it in. I just have to!*

It was a long week of waiting. To help me avoid the emotional turmoil, Cassandra waited day after day at the law school for the list to be published, while I stayed home and continued to study for the oral exams I hoped I would be able to take.

On the evening of the sixth day, Cassandra came home with a bouquet of flowers and a special dessert.

"Congratulations!" she cried. "You passed the written exams!"

"Really?" I exclaimed in disbelief, trying to contain my excitement.

"Yes. Here," she said, fishing a sheet of paper out of her purse. "I brought you a copy of the list so you could see."

I snatched the paper from her hands and quickly scanned the list, looking for my name.

"I am so proud of you, Virginia. You will make the best lawyer in Bucharest!" Cassandra beamed, wiping tears of joy from her eyes.

Basta, Virginia. I couldn't believe it. My name was actually there.

"I passed," I said quietly. Then louder, "I passed!" I was so excited, I ran right into Aunt Cassandra's arms and wrapped her in a giant hug. Before I knew it, we were both crying, laughing, and jumping up and down. I couldn't remember ever being happier than I was at that moment. And the fact that Cassandra shared so deeply in my joy made the moment even better.

As I hugged her tightly, I fought the urge to whisper the words that had been residing in my heart for days—*I wish you* were *my mother.*

CHAPTER 5

I do not fear. . . . I was born for this.

—JOAN OF ARC

"EXPLAIN TO ME, please, what *persona non grata* means."

I took a deep breath. It was the first day of oral examinations, and I was nervous but prepared.

"*Persona non grata*," I began, "refers to any Romanian citizen who—according to Communist rules and procedures—is considered to be unfaithful or unlawful, either by betraying the rule of silence established by the government, defying or speaking out publicly against the government or its leaders, interacting with foreigners without government approval, or communicating directly with Romania's known enemies."

As I recited the definition, it occurred to me that I was essentially describing anyone whose objective it was to speak the truth or act freely. It was common knowledge that those labeled as persona non grata were often ostracized by family and friends, and many simply "disappeared."

I wonder if Anna's parents were considered persona non grata. Perhaps that was why they were taken away. That's probably why Uncle Carol chose not to speak up as well. My musings were abruptly halted by one of my examiners.

"I hope *you* will never become persona non grata!" he joked.

So did I.

After several hours of being examined, I was exhausted but delighted. I had received perfect scores across the board. By the end of the week, the final list would be posted, and I would learn my fate—either a bright future with Aunt Cassandra in Bucharest or a dismal existence back in Techirghiol with Elena and Stephen.

Oh, please let me have passed.

On Friday, there was a multitude of people standing in the courtyard waiting for the list to be posted. You could feel the tension in the air. I couldn't even eat breakfast that morning for all the butterflies in my stomach. When the list was finally posted, it was mayhem. All around me, people were either cheering or crying, their dreams—like mine—either realized or dashed. Finally I made my way up to the board where the list was posted. I felt so dizzy from hunger and apprehension that I could barely think straight. I stepped closer, scanning the sheet of paper for my name. My heart was pounding in my ears.

Please be there. Please.

"Congratulations, Virginia!" I looked to my left. It was one of the girls who was in my group for the oral exams. "You made it!"

I did?

I turned back to the list, put my index finger to the sheet, and slowly traced a line downward until I hit my name. As soon as I saw it, a tremendous smile broke across my face, and without even thinking, I shouted out, "Victory! I passed! I passed!"

The butterflies in my stomach turned into fireworks. I was so euphoric that, had I known the words, I would have broken into song and dance like Gene Kelly in *Singin' in the Rain. What a glorious feeling—I'm happy again!*

I walked home on clouds, fighting the urge to hug everyone who came into my path.

"Aunt Cassandra!" I called as soon as I opened the door. "I passed! I passed!"

"Oh, Virginia! Congratulations!" She beamed, hugging and kissing me. "Tomorrow we will celebrate at Hanul lui Manuc!"

"But that's such an expensive restaurant," I countered. "And it's so famous. How will we even get in?"

"Oh, that won't be a problem," Cassandra said, smiling. "I made the reservation the week before you arrived in Bucharest."

I was astonished—and greatly touched. Aunt Cassandra believed in me even more than I believed in myself.

Why couldn't you have raised me? I thought. Aunt Cassandra had to be right around Elena's age, so she was definitely old enough to have a child my age. But as far as I knew, she had never married. For a moment, my heart saddened. *What a shame she never had a daughter of her own. She has so much love to give. That must be why she is so kind and loving toward me.*

That afternoon, as a special treat, Cassandra took me shopping again. This time she bought me perfume, makeup, and nail polish.

"I've never worn makeup before. Could you show me how to use it?"

"Of course!" she responded. "Now what color nail polish would you like?" she asked, directing me to a display of tiny bottles in every shade of pink, red, and purple imaginable.

"A simple red will be fine," I said, thinking of the beautiful red dress she had bought me earlier.

As Cassandra paid for our purchases, I began to worry. Classes wouldn't begin until September. Elena had agreed to let me stay in Bucharest while I prepared for and took my exams, but now that they were over, I would have to go back to Techirghiol for the remainder of the summer.

What will Elena make of my new clothing and makeup and nail polish? I wondered. *Will she let me keep them, or will she take them away?* I tried to block the thought from my mind. I still had one more day left with Cassandra, and I was determined to make the most of it. Besides, I would be back in Bucharest in two months. Perhaps I could leave my new things here with her for safekeeping. I'd just have to think of some way to explain why I was doing it. I had already sensed some animosity between Elena and Cassandra, and I didn't want to make it any worse. From what I could gather, something had happened many years ago—around the time I was born—that fractured their relationship, and things had never been the same since.

As soon as we walked through the door of Cassandra's home, the phone started to ring. Cassandra rushed to answer it while I headed to my room to start packing. I could hear Cassandra talking in the other room, but I couldn't make out what she was saying. I was too focused on what I should pack and what I should plan to leave behind. The dresses would surely be noticed. But I wondered if I could hide the nail polish and the makeup somehow, so I could practice applying them over the summer.

Just as I was rolling the nail polish bottle into a sock, Cassandra rushed into the room, her eyes wide with delight.

"That was your mother," she said.

Elena called? I thought. *Why didn't she ask to speak with me?*

"She said you could stay with me for the rest of the summer!"

I could hardly believe my ears. "Really?"

"Yes! Stop packing. You are staying right here." We met in an embrace.

Just then, the phone rang again. My heart sank.

Oh no, I thought. *Please don't let Elena have changed her mind.*

Moments later, Cassandra called me into the living room.

"Sit down for a minute," she said, patting the spot next to her on the sofa.

My feet felt like lead as I crossed the room. I sat next to her and held my breath, bracing for the worst.

"Radu didn't pass the law school exam," she said, looking straight into my eyes.

Oh, thank goodness. I exhaled, relief flooding my veins. But my relief was quickly replaced by guilt. Not so much that Radu had failed his exam, but that I had totally forgotten about him.

"Are you sure?" I asked.

"Yes. I checked the list myself, and then just in case I had missed something, I asked one of my friends to check too. That was her that called just now. I'm sorry, Virginia. He didn't pass."

I thought about this for a moment. On the one hand, I barely knew Radu. We'd had only one or two brief conversations during the exams. But I *had* agreed to see him again when he called last week. In a way, I reasoned, he was the only friend I had in Bucharest. "Should I call him?" I asked.

"Maybe it would be better to wait for him to call," she responded. I was actually a little relieved. I was so excited right now, it would be hard not to let that show. And I couldn't even imagine how I would feel had I not passed.

It turned out Cassandra was right. Radu did call later that week. We talked several times—mostly about benign things like the weather and things that were happening in town.

I had decided not to bring up law school or the exams unless he did first. And he did not.

After a few conversations, we agreed to meet for a walk in the park. I wasn't looking forward to it. Radu was very nice, and I liked him, but we were starting to run out of things to talk about. After all, our only real connection was through the exams. I could talk for hours about law school and my dreams of becoming an attorney, but those topics were off-limits with Radu. And to be frank, the weather in Bucharest wasn't all that interesting.

Regardless, we agreed to meet at 3:30 the next afternoon in front of the clock in town. I arrived first. Five minutes later, Radu still had not arrived. *I am sure he said 3:30 in front of the clock,* I thought, looking around the crowded street. I checked the clock again. 3:36. *Perhaps he changed his mind.*

Then, just as I was about to head back toward the bus depot, Radu's voice boomed from behind me.

"Here you are!" he said, lifting me up into the air.

His actions caught me completely off guard. "You're late," was all I could think to say.

"No, I wasn't," he said, setting me back down. "I was here the entire time, standing behind the clock watching you."

I felt my cheeks go red. "Well . . . do you want to walk in the park or don't you?" I said, straightening my dress.

"Of course," he said, smiling. "I'm sorry if I frightened you."

We took a few steps in silence.

"That's a very nice dress," he said, trying to catch my eye.

"Thank you," I responded, my eyes focused on the ground.

It was a beautiful day, and the park was alive with kids playing and lovers strolling hand in hand. Suddenly, I became self-conscious. What if Radu tried to take my hand? I had never dated a boy before. *I should have asked Cassandra about this,* I chided myself, casually moving ever so slightly away from Radu lest our hands accidentally touch.

Eventually we found a vacant bench, but instead of sitting down, we both just stood there, silently watching the people walking by or paddling in boats on the lake.

I couldn't stand the silence any longer. "How has your week been so far?"

"Terrible," he responded, looking down and kicking at the dirt. "My mom is killing me. She is so disappointed that I didn't pass the exams."

Finally, it was out. "I'm so sorry," I said, touching his arm. And before I knew it, I was crying—though why, I did not know. Embarrassed, I pulled a handkerchief from my purse, but before I could lift it to my face, Radu plucked it from my hand and gently began wiping the tears from my cheeks.

"Do you think you'll take the exams again?" I asked.

"Yes. But even if I pass, I will not be in the same year as you."

We stood in silence.

"Come on," he said, taking my hand. "The bus will be arriving soon."

We quietly walked back to town, lost in our own thoughts. *Should I offer to help him study?* I wondered. *It would be nice to have a friend here in Bucharest. Or would he be insulted or embarrassed if I offered to help?* I did not know much about dating or men, but I did know that they didn't like to feel inferior to women. I decided to apply Cassandra's earlier advice and wait for him to ask for help. Besides, soon I would have a lot of my own studying to do.

The following week, Radu called to tell me that he had taken a summer job helping some friends paint houses. When I told Cassandra, she suggested that I take Radu someplace nice to celebrate. "I know," she exclaimed. "I'll get you tickets for the matinee of the opera *La traviata*. You can wear one of your new dresses." She winked at me.

The afternoon of the matinee, I wore my red dress, accented with a black belt and my new red shoes, and Cassandra helped me apply some of the makeup she had purchased for me. I even wore a little bit of perfume.

"There," she said, looking over her finished work. "You look beautiful."

Just then, there was a knock at the door. It was Radu.

"Hi," he said cheerily. I couldn't believe my eyes. He was still dressed in his painting clothes, and he recked of turpentine. He even had yellow paint in his hair and streaked across his forehead.

"Are we still going to the opera?" I asked, my face a mask of confusion.

"Of course," he said matter-of-factly.

"You have got to be joking," I responded.

"Why?" he asked. "What's the matter?" His eyes hardened.

"So now that you're an elite law school student, you cannot be seen with a lowly worker—a proletarian—like me?"

I stared back at him, the anger in my eyes matching his own.

"What is wrong with me going to the opera dressed like this?" he continued, derision dripping from every word. "I am a blue-collar worker!"

What is he trying to prove? I wondered. I opened my mouth but decided it was best not to answer. I was too angry.

"Good-bye, Radu," I finally said, closing the door in disgust. *That's it,* I decided. *He can study on his own.*

That night, I wrote Radu a letter telling him I didn't want to see him anymore and asking him not to call on me again.

Still, that summer was the best summer of my life. I slept late; I had very few chores; and I had a wonderful time with Cassandra. She taught me how to bake bread and cookies and how to make chicken soup and stuffed cabbage rolls. I probably put on ten pounds over those months.

We discussed books and poetry, and she even took me to the opera, the ballet, and the symphony. By summer's end, I had seen *Swan Lake*, *A Midsummer Night's Dream*, *Romeo and Juliet*, *Carmen*, and *Madama Butterfly*. I swear, sometimes I thought I was dreaming. I had never felt so loved in my entire life.

Before I knew it, the summer was over, and classes were set to begin. Though I was prepared to move into the dormitory, Cassandra insisted that I stay with her.

"It would be so much nicer having your own room and

decent meals every night," she reasoned. Deep down, however, I knew the truth. Like me, she wasn't ready for us to part yet.

"I think you're right," I said. "I think I should stay here." Her eyes glistening with tears, she wrapped me in a warm and loving hug. *How nice,* I thought, *to finally feel wanted. To finally feel loved.*

CHAPTER 6

Life does not ask us what we want.
It presents us with options.

—THOMAS SOWELL

ONE SATURDAY I answered the phone, and to my surprise, it was Radu.

"Please don't hang up," he quickly blurted. "I have great news to tell you."

I waited. "Well . . . what is it?"

"I passed the night law school exam."

I was stunned. *Night law school? That's usually reserved for the* Securitate. *How in the world did he get in?* "Congratulations, Radu. That's wonderful!"

"Thank you." There was a pause. "I want to apologize for before. I was upset about failing my exams, and I am afraid I took it out on you." He sounded very sincere. "I've missed you so much," he continued. "Especially your beautiful smile. I hope we can be friends again."

"I hope so too," I said, surprising even myself. "So how are your classes going so far?"

"Good," he said. "But it's been hard to keep up. I still work during the day, and sometimes it's hard to focus late at night. Some nights, it's all I can do to keep my eyes open in class."

"I'm sorry," I said. And I was. Having been in school for several weeks now myself, I couldn't imagine working all day and then taking classes at night. Keeping all of that technical legal information straight was challenging enough when you were well rested. I couldn't imagine doing it after a full day's work. "Is there anything I can do to help?"

He paused. "Is there any way you would be willing to share some of your notes with me?" He sounded so sheepish. *Wow,* I thought. *That had to be a difficult thing for him to ask. Men are never supposed to ask for help from women.*

I considered it for a moment. "Of course, I'll share my notes with you." *Why not?* I figured. I had planned to help him study before anyway. Besides, even though I hated to admit it given our last interaction, I had missed him too.

We began meeting every other Saturday in the park. I would give him copies of my course notes, and we would discuss the material together. In effect, helping Radu helped me study too. Explaining my notes solidified the lessons in my mind. And it was wonderful having someone to prepare for tests and quizzes with. On top of everything else, Radu began to become a real friend, and he never had another angry outburst like the one he'd had the afternoon of the opera. Until . . .

One day I was talking with four of my classmates about our project for contracts class.

"Mosu, you start first and pretend you're initiating the contract between us," I said.

"I'm your man," replied the six-foot-tall, muscular colleague at my side.

"Good. Now we need someone to play the role of mediator."

"I'll be the mediator," Nina responded.

"Great . . ." Before I could say another word, Radu suddenly came up from behind and kissed me. I felt my face flush with embarrassment. "Excuse me," I said to my classmates. "This will only take a minute." I pulled Radu aside, out of earshot from the rest of the group. "What did you do that for?" I hissed.

"Mosu likes you," he hissed back. "I have been watching him."

"Don't be ridiculous," I countered. "He is just a friend."

There was fire in Radu's eyes. "Do you know he is the future Gypsy king of Romania?"

"What?"

"Well, he is," Radu continued, grasping my arm tightly. "And he wants to make you his queen."

"You're being irrational," I said, pulling free from him. I glanced behind me and saw my friends watching us. Nina shot me a look that said, *Do you need help?* I was mortified. I quickly shook my head no, trying to fight back the color in my cheeks. I turned back to Radu. "I think you should go," I said, taking a step back. "From now on, I will leave my notes with the librarian."

"What? You're breaking up with me again?" he whispered cynically.

"Please go," I said, turning my back to him. "You've embarrassed me enough for one day." And with that, I walked back over to my friends, leaving Radu standing there with a quizzical look on his face.

"Where were we?" I said, trying to distract them from the scene that had just taken place.

"Is that your boyfriend, Virginia?" Nina asked. "He's cute!"

"No," I spat. "He's not. He's one of the students attending evening classes. Sometimes I share my notes with him."

"Ooooh," cooed Nina. "Is he one of those *Securitate* guys? I hear they have a lot of power! Tell me, Virginia, does he have a classmate I could lend *my* notes to?"

"No, Nina," I said, exasperated. "He is *not* a *Securitate* guy. He's just a boy I met this summer. Now, please, let's get back to work."

Radu and I kept our distance for several weeks after that.

*

For the most part, I genuinely enjoyed my classes. My favorites, though, were civil and criminal law. They had a vocabulary all their own, and as I became more and more fluent in it, I started to feel like an actual attorney. I even started talking like an attorney outside of class, which at times made things a bit awkward.

"The family code—in fact, the entire Section Six—covers the division of property, including division during divorce proceedings," I blurted out one day during a luncheon visit with one of Cassandra's friends, who was going through a divorce.

"Virginia is a law student," Cassandra explained to the table of stunned friends and acquaintances. They all glanced at each other briefly and then at me. Then the floodgates opened.

"What is the sentence for stealing a piece of bread?" one asked.

"Can I create my own company?" asked another. "What would the punishment be if I did?"

I was in over my head.

"I don't know . . . exactly . . . the punishment for that," I stammered. "But I know for sure that you cannot operate a private company." I was fairly sure, at least. Glancing around the table at a sea of expectant faces, I thought it best to qualify myself. "Actually, I just started my criminal and civil law classes this semester," I said, blushing. I noticed the light going out of their eyes as they leaned back in their seats. I glanced at Cassandra, who was smirking at me slightly, and I felt her hand pat my thigh under the table.

To her credit, Cassandra never chided me for acting the role of an attorney before being ready for it. In fact, she was my greatest champion. Whenever I prepared for class presentations or trial competitions, Cassandra served as my audience, patiently listening to my arguments, always applauding when I was finished, and cheerfully assuring me that I would be an excellent attorney someday.

*

One crisp autumn morning, I opened my windows, and—invigorated by the fresh air—called out to Cassandra, "It is going to be a great day."

I smelled breakfast long before she brought it to me—a cup of coffee, two boiled eggs, and a banana muffin. As soon as I finished my breakfast, I settled in at my desk to study. A few hours later, the doorbell rang. Since Cassandra was busy in the kitchen, I got up and opened the door to a handsome, middle-aged man. "Good afternoon, sir," I said. "What can I do for you?"

He stared at me with big, blue eyes. "My name is John." He looked at me as though he had seen a ghost. "Wow! You look *just* like your mother when she was your age." I instinctively took a step back. I had seen pictures of Elena as a child, and we looked nothing alike. If anything, I looked much more like Cassandra.

"I'm sorry," he explained, shaking his head. "But the resemblance is so uncanny." Then he reached into his vest pocket and handed me a slip of paper. "Here. I have a note for your mother."

Before I could take the note from him, I felt a hand on my shoulder pulling me back. It was Cassandra. She also looked as though she had seen a ghost.

"Ah!" the man exclaimed. "Here's your mother."

Cassandra's eyes burned like fire. "Go to your room, Virginia," she growled. "Now!" I had never seen her like this. I knew better than to fight with her, so I quietly slunk back to my desk, where I pretended to study.

I could hear them discussing something in hushed yet angry tones, but I couldn't make out the words. *Who is this man? Why does his presence upset Cassandra so? What does he know about my mother?*

Moments later, the door slammed shut and Cassandra appeared in my room. She paced back and forth furiously, staring at the carpet, her hands knotted into fists.

"Don't you ever open that door again, do you hear me?" she said, scowling.

"No. Of course not," I replied, terrified by this sudden change in her demeanor. She stopped pacing for a moment and looked at me. Fury softened to sadness as her eyes glazed over with tears. She opened her mouth as though she wanted to say something, but then she caught herself, bit her lip, and hurried out into the hall, stifling a sob.

My heart felt heavy and bruised. *Should I go after her? What did that man say to get her so upset?* I heard the click of Cassandra's bedroom door. I stepped out into the hall and thought for a moment about knocking, but then decided it might be best to wait and let her calm down first.

A few hours later, Cassandra and I shared a painfully quiet and lonely lunch. Whoever that man was and whatever that note said, it had upset her greatly. She could barely look at me. Come morning, her eyes were still red with tears.

The episode continued to haunt me throughout my classes that day. Even in my favorite class—criminal law—my body was there, but my mind was not. When I returned home that evening, I found food waiting for me on the kitchen table and a note from Cassandra asking me not to disturb her.

In our family, when an adult did not want to talk about something, a young person was not allowed to ask questions. So for the next few days, I tried to act as though nothing had happened. It was not easy. I missed Cassandra's smile, her laugh, and her upbeat nature. I missed hearing her singing to herself and her going out of her way to hug me. It was as though all the joy had been sucked out of the house, and in its place only coldness and misery remained. Even the fresh flowers Cassandra brought to my room every day looked dead to me.

Many nights, I cried myself to sleep. The pain and lone-liness were overwhelming. When I looked in the mirror, all I could hear were John's words: "You look exactly like your mother! Ah! Here's your mother!"

My stomach fluttered. *Could Cassandra be my mother?* I studied my reflection. We did look a lot alike. People were always confusing us for mother and daughter. And now that I thought about it, Cassandra never did correct anyone when they commented on it. I tried to process the facts like an attorney. *Elena and Cassandra had a huge falling out shortly after I was born. They rarely speak, and when the family does go to visit her, I am never allowed to come. I don't look like anyone in my family, and Elena always treats me as though I'm an outsider. Cassandra, on the other hand, has treated me like a daughter since I arrived.* And of course there was the physical resemblance. *But if I were Cassandra's daughter, why wouldn't she say something? Why would she possibly want to keep that a secret? And if she is my mother, who—and where—is my father?*

Once again, it seemed, the truth eluded me.

*

The weeks passed, and then one snowy morning while Cassandra was out, the telephone rang, and I answered.

"Hello. May I please speak to Virginia?" It was a man's voice. It sounded vaguely familiar, but I could not place it.

"This is Virginia," I replied. "Who is this?"

"It's better that you not know," he stated calmly. As if sensing my trepidation, he quickly begged me not to hang up. Usually I refused to talk with strangers, but something about his voice captivated me. So I listened as he talked about himself and his work, as if he wanted me to know all about him. He spoke with a certain familiarity, as though he knew me, but despite my repeated requests, he refused to tell me his name.

"You can call me Paul, but that is not my name, Virginia," he finally acquiesced. When he spoke again, he sounded apprehensive. "Please make sure you don't tell your mother about this call," he pleaded. "I am not sure Cassandra wants us to talk."

"Okay," I responded after a long pause. *Why does he refer to Cassandra as my mother?* It was then that I recognized the voice. It was the man who had appeared at the door weeks ago. *Who is this man?*

"I have to go now, Virginia," he finally said. "But I will call you again soon."

"Okay. Good-bye, Paul. It was nice talking with you."

"Good-bye, Virginia. And remember, not a word to Cassandra."

I hung up the phone more confused than ever. My mind was racing. *What is going on?*

True to my word, I did not mention the call to Cassandra. And after several weeks had passed with no word from Paul, I figured that whoever he was, he had found whatever solace he was looking for in that call and moved on.

Then one day, out of the blue, the phone rang.

"Hi, Virginia!" I recognized his voice instantly. "How is school going? Are you keeping up with your studies?"

"Yes, thank you." It was strange. He seemed so comfortable talking with me. And he seemed to know a great deal about me and my classes.

"You know, if you go to the library early in the morning, there will be a better selection of books, and the librarians will be more available to help answer your questions."

"I know, but that's not always possible," I countered. *Wait. How does he know when I study?* Before I could interject, he broke back in.

"Can I read you something?" he asked.

"Yes."

He began to read in a foreign language. I think it was Hebrew. Naturally, I didn't understand a word, though I suspected it was something from the Bible.

Our conversations went on for three months. He would ask me about my classes and give me advice about my studies, and then he would share his favorite poems or Hebrew readings. In some ways, he reminded me of Stephen after he had been drinking—very warm and fatherly, though I wasn't always certain what he was saying. Always he closed our conversations with the request that I not tell Cassandra. And always I honored his request. Over the months, I had grown to enjoy our conversations—to look forward to them, even. With Radu out of the picture and Cassandra still awkwardly distant, it was nice having someone friendly to talk to.

Then one day, the tone of our conversation changed. Paul seemed sad, as though he were choking back tears.

"I have enjoyed talking with you so much, Virginia. You brought what was missing in my life." He took a deep breath. "But it is better that I not call you anymore. Please know I will never forget you," he said softly. "Good-bye, Virgina."

Then he hung up, and a dial tone filled the silence.

I never heard from him again. And I never did tell Cassandra about our calls. Paul had vanished from my life as mysteriously as he had entered it. But I had a feeling that his tender voice, his advice, and his poems would stay with me forever.

73

CHAPTER 7

*I am not a product of my
circumstances. I am a product of
my choices.*

—STEPHEN R. COVEY

BY THE TIME MY midterm exams were over, I was a wreck and
ready for spring break. Cassandra and I were comfortable
together again, and I was energized by her plans for our first
spring break together. She wanted us to see several musicals
in Bucharest and to visit two old castles located a few hours
away in the mountains.

That spring break gave me a unique opportunity to go
on a vacation for the first time in my life—to see mountains full of wild animals and delicate flowers, to visit famous
museums, and to enjoy picnics along the highway. Cassandra
taught me how to relax and stop worrying and to find something to laugh about and enjoy in everything around me.

"Look, Virginia. Do you see that bird over there?" Cassandra said, pointing to a bright yellow bird bobbing from branch to branch in a nearby tree. "Just listen to the beautiful song it is singing. That is the sound of relaxation. You work too hard for someone your age. You need to learn how to let go and enjoy life more."

She was right. I wanted to relax; I just didn't know how. The truth is, I had never learned. Up until then, my entire life had been spent working—doing chores around the house or chasing down tourists in the square. *How odd,* I thought, *to have to learn how to have fun.* Then again, "having fun" wasn't exactly a top priority of the Communist regime.

Regardless, I returned home rejuvenated and ready to finish my first year of law school. Near the end of May, I received approval to do an internship with the attorney general's office in Bucharest. I was ecstatic. Each case I worked on was an opportunity for me to apply what I had learned in school—except perhaps one.

The assignment involved examining a body at the local morgue—an assignment, I was told, no girl had ever finished before. I knew that going to the morgue would be difficult, but I was determined to be the first female student to succeed. So that afternoon, an assistant from the attorney general's office, a group of five male colleagues, and I went to the morgue. On the table lay a young soldier's naked body, riddled with bullets. Our assignment was to examine the body and determine how he died.

When the morgue worker helped us turn the body

over—all the while munching on a sandwich—I was shocked by his callousness. I was also terrified at being so close to a dead, naked body. I felt sick to my stomach. I wanted to run away, but I wanted to show my male colleagues that a woman *could* do this. I survived the afternoon, but when I got home that night, I locked myself in my room and cried for hours. The image and the smell of the morgue haunted me so terribly that I couldn't eat meat for more than a month.

Not all of my assignments were that grisly, though. I also got to accompany other attorneys when they interrogated prisoners in the city jail; I got to work on several projects in the criminal lab; and I helped prepare oral arguments for trial depositions. Dead bodies and a brief stint as a vegetarian aside, it was a wonderful learning experience, and as the summer drew to a close, I couldn't wait to get back to school and get one step closer to my ultimate goal.

*

One evening as I was walking home from work, I heard screaming coming from Cassandra's house. When I got closer, I recognized the voice as Elena's. *What on earth is she doing here?* The door was locked, so I rang the doorbell. When Cassandra opened the door, her eyes were red with tears.

"Virginia, I need you to go for a walk," she said, blocking the entrance. "Come back in an hour or so. Your mother is here, and we need to talk."

I craned my neck to try to see over Cassandra's shoulder. "But . . ."

Before I could even get a sentence out, Elena yelled from inside, "I am taking her back home! Her place is in Techirghiol. I am the one who raised her—not you! She should be home helping me! All this nonsense with law school is over!"

Tears sprang to my eyes, and a knot formed in my stomach. *What?* "No!" I said, frantically grabbing at Cassandra's shoulders. "She can't do this. I can't go back home. I can't quit law school. She can't make me!"

Cassandra grasped my hands, leaned closer, and whispered, "Hush. It's okay, Virginia. Go for a walk. I'll talk to your mother." She forced a smile and nodded at me as if to say that everything was going to be okay, but the look in her eyes said otherwise.

I spent the next hour walking around Bucharest in a fog, my eyes glassy with tears. *Why now?* I wondered. Elena had not reached out to me once the entire time I had been here. She hadn't even asked to speak to me the day she called to tell Cassandra I could stay for the summer. It was almost as though she sensed my happiness from afar and decided she had to put an end to it. *That sounds like something Elena would do. But why now?* The question haunted me all the way back to Cassandra's house. When I went inside, I was greeted by silence.

Elena was gone, and Cassandra looked like another person entirely. The light had gone out of her eyes, and her once cheerful face was now a vacant mask of sorrow.

"Cassandra?" I asked. "What happened? Where is Elena?"

She stared at me glassy eyed and opened her mouth as if to say something and then sighed deeply, stood up, and walked quietly into her bedroom and closed the door. I instinctively took two steps forward but stopped when I heard the click of the lock.

I wanted to go talk to her—to find out what had happened. When I pressed my ear to her door, I could hear her crying. Suddenly, I felt like the soldier we had examined in the morgue—cold and lifeless, with nothing but holes where my heart used to be.

Cassandra sobbed throughout the night. I knew, because I lay awake in the next room listening to her. And with each hour that passed, I became more and more resigned to the fact that I would soon be leaving Bucharest—whether I wanted to or not.

The next morning as she prepared our breakfast, a stoic Cassandra informed me, "You cannot live here anymore. You need to pack all of your belongings and go find a room in one of the law school's dorms. You cannot return here—even for a visit."

"Why? What have I done?"

"Just be happy that you get to stay in school, Virginia." She looked exhausted and defeated.

I was at a complete loss. *How did this happen? Just yesterday everything was so wonderful.* Tears stung at my eyes and throat. *How could Cassandra* let *this happen? Why didn't she fight back?* Then I realized that she had. I got to stay in

Bucharest. I got to stay in law school. Given Elena's fury yesterday, those were two major victories—victories I was certain Cassandra had fought hard to win. Nevertheless, they came at a devastating loss. The past year had been the happiest of my life. Cassandra had shown me more love, more affection, more kindness, and more support in the past twelve months than Stephen and Elena had shown me in my entire life. I could feel the anger forming like a fist in my chest. To have that mercilessly yanked away with no notice and for no apparent reason was . . . my mind struggled to find the right word.

Communist.

That afternoon I packed up all of my things, and Cassandra called a taxi to take me to campus. As the driver loaded my bags into the trunk, I turned to say something, *anything*, to Cassandra. I wanted to thank her for everything she had done for me. To beg her one last time to ignore Elena's demands and let me stay. But when I opened my mouth, nothing came out. Instead, I reached over and embraced Cassandra, tears running down my cheeks and dampening the neckline of her blouse. I could feel her trembling as she hugged me.

The driver opened the door of the taxi and cleared his throat.

"Good-bye, Virginia," Cassandra stammered, slowly backing away. "I'm so happy I got to know you. I know you'll be a brilliant attorney someday." She forced a smile.

"Thank you, Aunt Cassandra," I managed. "For everything."

The driver cleared his throat again.

"Go," Cassandra whispered. Ducking my head, I slid into the backseat, and the driver slammed the door. As we pulled away from the curb, I turned and watched Cassandra—and the only happiness I had ever known—fade slowly into the distance.

When we finally arrived at the dorm, the driver put all of my bags on the sidewalk and left. Seconds after he drove away, I saw the sign on the dormitory entrance: Closed for Renovation. *Perfect. Now what am I supposed to do?*

As I was contemplating my next move, the dean happened to walk by.

"Hi, Virginia. Are you going home?" he asked, eyeing my luggage.

Home. The tears I had fought back in the taxi resurfaced. "I don't have a home, sir," I sobbed.

Concern immediately registered on his face. "Let's go back to my office and talk," he said, picking up my bags.

Upon hearing my story, he solemnly stated, "In my eighteen years as dean of this law school, I have never had a situation like this. Don't worry, Virginia. I'm personally going to make sure you have a place to stay."

True to his word, later that afternoon, the dean signed a waiver allowing me to stay in the dorm while the renovation continued. He even gave me some money for food.

"I know it's not ideal," he said to me, "but at least you will have a roof over your head and food in your stomach until the semester begins." As I turned to leave his office, he stopped me one last time. "I'm sorry, Virginia. I wish I could do more."

"Thank you, sir. And please, do not feel guilty. You have done a great deal," I assured him. And he had. In the midst of all the turmoil of the past twenty-four hours, it was a tremendous comfort knowing that I still had at least one ally looking out for me.

I carefully picked my way toward the dorm entrance, negotiating between sheets of steel, paint cans, wood, machinery, and several workers who were puzzled by my presence there. When I found my assigned room on the third floor, I was struck by how spartan it was. There was one iron bed with a mattress but no sheets, a tiny closet, and a table with one chair. There was no telephone, no sink, and no bathroom. The restroom was down the hall, along with the doorless shower room. *How am I supposed to take a shower with all of these male construction workers around?* I wondered. I thought briefly about speaking with the dean, but he had already been so generous, and I did not want to appear ungrateful. *I suppose I could shower late at night when the building is empty,* I thought, a shiver going down my spine.

As I lay on my bare mattress that evening, the silence was rife with unspoken questions: *What drove Elena to travel all the way to Bucharest and demand my immediate return? Elena never wanted me around when I was growing up; why did she suddenly crave my presence now? And why did Cassandra seem so powerless to stop her? Could it have something to do with the disagreement they'd had all those years ago?*

Once again, the truth eluded me. I felt like a puppet on a string, manipulated by forces I could not see, directed by logic I did not understand. My future—like the empty dormitory—looked scary and intimidating.

Just past midnight that first night, I was awakened by the sound of somebody trying to open my door.

"Who's there?" I called out, not really wanting to know the answer. Straining in the silence, I could hear the faint sound of laughter and the continued jiggling of the doorknob. My heart in my throat, I jumped out of bed and quickly pushed the table in front of the door. Then I opened the window. As I swung a leg over the sill, preparing to jump, I paused and stared at the table, looking for signs of movement. There was none. I listened carefully but could hear nothing. The rattling and the laughter had stopped. *Perhaps it was just one of the workers trying to frighten me as a joke,* I reasoned. I spent the remainder of the night warily standing in front of the window, thinking about how I would definitely *not* be taking a shower in the morning.

I thought of reporting the incident to the dean, but I was afraid that if I did, he might rescind his offer to let me stay there. If I were to be kicked out of the dorm, I would have no choice but to return to Techirghiol—a prospect that frightened me even more than my late-night visitor. So that afternoon I put together a plan. I would always return from work while it was still daylight; I would barricade myself in my room with plenty of books to read; and I would not use the shower or the restroom in the dorm. Instead, I kept a big jar in my room to use as a toilet, and I used a sink in the public restroom to wash my hair and brush my teeth. Washing my hair in the sink of a public restroom was a disgusting, degrading experience. I had to wash with cold water as fast as possible, keeping my eyes opened the entire time in case anyone came in. I could not bear the thought of people assuming that I was either a "bad girl" or a runaway. I was a law student. I was supposed to be one of the elite. To be caught washing in a public restroom would be an embarrassment to both the school and the government. I flashed back to my oral exams. I was just one misstep away from being persona non grata.

A couple of weeks later, one of the attorneys I was interning for asked me to help him with a new case. I read the facts of the case and looked at each picture, then dropped the file on the floor. The case was about a woman who was raped and murdered in a restroom not far from where I had washed my hair that morning. From that day on, I used community showers at swimming pools to bathe—always making sure there were other people around—and I counted the days until the new school year would start and the dorm would once again be filled with students.

*

That summer brought with it not only the return of Elena, but the return of Radu as well. Though we had not parted on good terms, my recent change of circumstances had left me desperately in need of a friend. And in fairness, his intermittent bouts of jealousy aside, I genuinely did enjoy Radu's company. He visited often, bringing me food and, sometimes, a little extra companionship in the form of his dog, Gypsy.

"I brought you a salami sandwich," he said one evening. "In case you didn't have anything for dinner," he quickly added. Though the dean had graciously given me some money at the start of the summer, by late August my food budget had been stretched to its limits, and for several weeks now—aside from the occasional treats Radu would bring—I had been subsisting on little more than a bagel and half a container of yogurt per day.

"Thank you," I said, taking the sandwich. "But you don't have to keep doing this. Your mother would be very upset if she knew."

"Don't be foolish," he said. "Besides, after the way I treated you last semester, it's the least I can do. Now you better start eating that sandwich before Gypsy does," he joked.

We both laughed as I dug into my sandwich while Gypsy stood at my feet and watched, her tongue lapping at her nose and lips.

"Come on," Radu said, standing and reaching for my hand. "Let's walk across the street to the park." I slid my hand into his and stood, and together we made our way to the park. It was nice being with Radu. So much of my summer had been spent living in fear—jumping at every sound that echoed through the empty halls and assigning horrifying visages to the shadows that played along the walls. Having him close by made me feel protected—safe.

When Gypsy began to get restless, we returned to the women's dormitory. Despite the fact that I was its sole inhabitant, Radu was not allowed to come inside. Instead, he walked me to the door, leaned in, and gently kissed me good-night.

"I'll stay here until you get to your room," he whispered. "Make sure you lock the door, and wave to me from the window so I will know you're safe." Then he kissed me again—this time longer.

"Good night, Virginia."

"Good night, Radu." I gave him one last peck on the cheek before rushing into the building. Moments later, I pulled aside the curtain and looked out my window to find Radu and Gypsy looking up at me from the street. I waved and blew them both a kiss. Radu pretended to reach out and snatch it from the air. His smile was the last thing I saw as the curtain fell back into place.

*

Nobody was happier than I was when school started. At last I had roommates and neighbors, and the once vacant dorm was now full of life. The construction workers had gone, and I could finally use the restrooms and take a nice hot shower anytime I wanted. It was sheer heaven—until Elena came back.

My roommates and I had gone to the library to work on a class project, and while we were out, Elena showed up at the dorm office, demanding access to my room. Assuming she had brought me something as a surprise, the receptionist gave her the key. I got a surprise all right. She took almost all my clothes, leaving me with just one black and one navy skirt, one pair of red slacks, two T-shirts, and one pair of shoes— my entire wardrobe for the next three years of law school.

My final three years of school were as predictable as my wardrobe. I stayed in the dorm every summer, spring, and Christmas break, studying morning, noon, and night, and when all was said and done, I graduated in the top ten of my class.

Radu and I continued to date, and shortly after graduation, we were married in a simple civil ceremony. Elena was invited but did not attend. Radu's parents did not know what to make of this. How does one justify not attending her own daughter's wedding?

In addition to Radu's parents, our entire guest list comprised ten of our mutual friends from school, one of our professors, and—of course—Cassandra. I wore a delicate pink dress and white high-heeled shoes, and Radu was dressed in a black suit, a white shirt, and a black tie. It was a simple yet beautiful ceremony.

Nine months later, our daughter, Anca, was born, followed two years later by Andreea. After more than twenty years of feeling like an outsider, I finally had a family of my own. I also had a law degree. *From here on out,* I declared to myself, *there will be no more mysteries—no more lies. From this moment on, my life will be dedicated to pursuing and speaking the truth, no matter the cost.*

CHAPTER 8

This truth is incontrovertible. Panic may resent it,
ignorance may deride it, malice may distort it,
but there it is.

—WINSTON CHURCHILL

WHILE BEING A LAWYER under the Communist regime did make me part of the "privileged" class, I really didn't consider myself privileged at all—at least not compared to most of my classmates. Many of them had parents who were high-ranking officials within the Communist government, and as such, they typically had chauffeurs picking them up from school, and they would often travel to Rome, Paris, or London.

Take my friend Farida, for example. She was from a small town called Giurgiu, located roughly forty miles south of Bucharest. Her father was the mayor, which made Farida part of the elite. As her father advanced in his political career, Farida—coincidentally—got better grades and more political job offers. At graduation, she became an attorney for the *Securitate*, and as part of her graduation package, she received a furnished house, a new car, and approval to travel outside Romania. We, on the other hand, lived with Radu's parents in Bucharest for two years. And whenever we needed to travel for work, we took the bus or the train.

Shortly after graduation, I was sent to Farida's town, Giurgiu, to represent a government-owned chemical company. The law office was tiny, and the city itself was miserable. The people were like the walking dead. They had no joy, no direction. Everyone was just trying to survive. The mood of the people was in many respects a reflection of the town itself. Once a thriving industrial area, Giurgiu was all but destroyed by Ceaușescu's wife, Elena. Having been granted a degree in chemistry (about which she knew nothing; it later came out that a number of real scientists had done Elena's course work for her), Elena had taken Giurgiu under her wing and slowly but surely, through her own incompetence, driven virtually all of its companies—and with them, the economy—into the dirt. And as usual, terrified of speaking out against the regime, the people stood by and said nothing. Actually, that is not entirely true. No matter how much the economy deteriorated under Elena's hand, the newspapers always had glowing things to say about our great dictator's wife and her "brilliant" business acumen.

Life as an attorney at that company—one of the most devastating Communist experiments ever under Elena Ceaușescu's destructive hands—was unbearable. Not only did the factory produce volumes of pollution, but workers had to endure extremely dangerous conditions. Some got sick, became paralyzed, or even died—with no insurance or benefits to help them or their families. My job was basically to rubber-stamp whatever ridiculous rules and regulations the government wanted to enforce. It was horrible, and I hated it.

About a month into the job, I was approached by a fellow attorney who invited me to apply for a position with the bar association in Giurgiu. It was a risky move. On the one hand, I was eager to get out on my own, away from any government ties. However, as an independent attorney, I would have to find my own clients and create my own salary. And fifty percent of my income would go to the government. As an attorney for the government-owned chemical company, I would have an assured position and a salary I could keep. But my job was to rubber-stamp government rules. The decision was simple, yet unsatisfying.

A week later, I walked into the Giurgiu Bar Association conference hall to meet my new colleagues. The majority of them were much older—and men—and the women looked suspicious, possibly even a little bitter. Finally my eyes stopped on a friendly face. When I smiled, the woman approached me. She was a tiny woman who walked with a cane.

"Hello. You must be Virginia," she began. "My name is Vera. Vera Popescu."

"It's so nice to meet you, Vera," I replied.

"You'll have to pardon the cane," she continued. "I'm afraid I have some back problems."

"No—not at all. Would you prefer to sit down?" I replied, scanning the room for a chair.

"Better yet," she responded, "why don't we go out for lunch, so we can talk and get to know each other better?"

No sooner had we sat down to lunch than Vera began sharing her entire story with me—and what a story it was!

"I was much older than you when I started out in this profession," she said. "Everyone expected me to fail. My parents were the only ones who believed in me, so I studied as hard as I could to make them proud," she continued.

"While I was in law school, I started experiencing excruciating pain in my back. It got so bad that even walking became difficult. So my parents took me to see a variety of doctors and specialists. One recommended an experimental spine-strengthening device that the government was testing. Unfortunately, the procedure did more harm than good, leaving me with a permanent curve in my spine. That's why I have to use a cane to walk," she explained, gesturing toward the wooden cane resting against the table.

"That's terrible," I said. "Were you and your family compensated at all for what happened?"

She stifled a laugh. "Of course not. Not only that, but we were strictly forbidden to speak about the incident or else . . . well, you know," she said, giving me a knowing look.

I did know. I stared down at my plate in frustration. This

system was so unfair. I could feel tears burning in the back of my throat.

"Don't worry, Virginia," Vera said. "You'll be just fine. You're young, but that will be an obstacle only if you let it. I believe in you, and I will help you—*as long as you are teachable.*" She emphasized those last six words.

I looked across the table at her. If she could find a way to survive in spite of everything she had been through, then so could I.

"Thank you, Vera," I said. "It's an honor to know that you will be by my side. I have wanted to be an attorney my entire life, and I promise I will do my very best."

"I like your enthusiasm," she responded. Then, taking a sip from her water glass, she added, "You'll need it."

Despite her frail appearance, Vera turned out to be one of the strongest people I had ever met. Her back may have been curved, but her confidence always made her seem like the tallest person in the room. I often noticed people looking down on her, and sometimes children would stare at her in the street. But she never complained or let it get to her. She had a self-assuredness that radiated from within, and she was always extremely well prepared, which quickly won the respect of even the most corrupt adversaries. They tried to bribe her into dropping cases and clients that the government did not like with promises of visits to London and Paris to meet with medical specialists about her condition, but she never folded. She saw through their tricks and wanted no part in their deceit. And for that, I admired her greatly.

Though I enjoyed learning under Vera, I knew I would not be able to stay in Giurgiu for long. Though the town was rebuilding and growing, housing was both limited and expensive. Radu and I both knew that if we wanted to have any chance at a future, we would have to find work in Bucharest. Not only did Bucharest have better and more affordable food, housing, shopping centers, entertainment, hospitals, and schools; there were also more opportunities for advancement.

So I applied to the Bucharest Bar Association. Because I was young and still relatively inexperienced, before they would accept me, I had to explain how I was going to survive in the capital.

"I started my career in Giurgiu," I began. "And as you can see from my recommendations, I did very well."

"That's true, Mrs. Prodan, but this is Bucharest," one of the members shot back. "We already have too many attorneys, and many of the younger ones are struggling to get by."

I held my ground. "I am a hard worker, and I know how to gain people's trust." They seemed unmoved. "I did well in school too. Just look at my grades."

A few of them flipped through my application to review my transcripts. Suddenly, one of them, an older gentleman, looked up and locked eyes with me.

"By any chance, did your last name used to be Basta?"

"Yes," I responded. "It was." *Where is he going with this?* I wondered.

"You may not remember me," he continued. "My name is Mihai Irimescu. You went to school with my daughter, Rodica."

I froze. I *had* gone to school with Rodica. During our second year of law school, Rodica had tried to commit suicide. One Friday afternoon after classes had ended, she took an entire bottle of Tylenol and collapsed on the bathroom floor. She had figured nobody would find her until the following week, but that evening, I happened to stop by the restroom and found her. I called an ambulance, and she was taken to the hospital in time to have her stomach pumped. Eventually, she returned to school, graduated, and went on to become a successful prosecutor.

"Yes. I remember Rodica well," I said, smiling slightly. He held my gaze for a moment, and then spoke.

"Several years ago, Mrs. Prodan saved my daughter's life." He went on to tell them the entire story. When he finished, the room was silent. "I always dreamed of having my daughter, Rodica, working by my side as an attorney, but she decided to become a prosecutor like her mother," he continued. "Virginia, I would be happy to train you until you are ready to practice on your own."

I was stunned. I had almost completely forgotten about Rodica. What were the odds that her father would be on the committee? My mind raced. On the one hand, I would be a fool to turn this opportunity down. And yet I wanted to be accepted on my own merit, not as a thank-you for a past deed. As if sensing my hesitancy, Mihai locked eyes with me again and said, "This is by no means a way of paying you back for saving my daughter's life." Then he addressed the rest of the group. "Virginia's record speaks for itself.

I believe she will become a great attorney, and I would be honored to help."

The committee accepted me on the spot.

Several weeks later, Radu also secured a position in Bucharest, and we took a spacious apartment in an affluent part of town near the American embassy.

By all outward appearances, we seemed to have everything. As attorneys, we made enough money to hire a maid and pay people to take our place in line to buy food and gas, and when our daughters were born, we were able to bring in a nanny to stay with them while we were at work. We even vacationed at the Black Sea in the summer and skied in the mountains in the winter.

But none of these privileges could overcome the stifling Communist oppression that seemed to permeate the very air we breathed.

Why aren't we allowed to know anything about the outside world? If America and the capitalist system are so horrible, why does our government restrict our access to direct information about it? Why are only "loyal Communists" allowed to travel outside Romania? What is it they do not want us to see?

After working with Mihai for a year, I decided I was ready to strike out on my own. I had learned a great deal, both from him and from Vera before him, and I was anxious to begin securing my own clients and trying my own cases.

My first solo case was a pro bono project that was riddled with complications. My client, Anton Sasu, a second-year student at the University of Bucharest, had been accused of deliberately burning his student Communist Party ID card. Prior to our court date, I visited him in jail.

"I was celebrating the end of my first year, and for fun, I decided to burn my old school pants and a few other items. I had no idea my ID card was in the pocket," he explained.

"Who was there with you?" I asked.

"Nobody," he replied. "But I told a neighbor and a few of my classmates."

"If it was an accident, why did you say that you did it on purpose?"

"I was told by the police that it would be better to admit it," he said, avoiding the gaze of the police officer seated beside him.

I also spoke with Anton's parents. At first, they confirmed their son's story, but after an unexpected "visit" from the police, they retracted their statements.

"You need to go back to the police and tell them the truth," I implored them.

They exchanged concerned glances. "Can they arrest us for that? We still have four kids at home."

"No, I don't think so," I replied. Though to be honest, I wasn't entirely sure. There was one thing I was certain of, though. "If you don't tell the truth, Anton will likely go to jail." When I left them that day, I had no idea how they would respond. As a parent myself, I couldn't imagine turning my back on my child. But the *Securitate* could be a very formidable force.

The day before the trial, I checked with the police, but Anton's parents had not retracted their altered testimonies.

I was extremely disappointed, both in Anton's parents and in the system that had put them—and their son—in this position. Under Romanian law, there was no "innocent until proven guilty"; the burden was on the defendant to prove his or her innocence. And with both Anton and his parents' succumbing to pressure from the *Securitate* to claim intentionality for what was clearly an accidental act, defending him was going to be virtually impossible—unless I could convince them to tell the truth.

Maybe seeing their son in a yellow jumpsuit will help persuade them to tell the truth, I reasoned. *Then again, they might start thinking about their other children and cave under the pressure again.* Given their previous response, I wasn't convinced Anton's parents could be counted on.

I could tell the court what Anton and his parents told me about being coerced into retracting their original statements, I thought. *But, if I do, and Anton and his parents don't stand up for themselves, the prosecutor could accuse* me *of coercing the witnesses to change their testimonies.* If that were to happen, the police could arrest me on the spot, and I could be disbarred. No matter how I looked at it, there was only one way out. Anton and his parents would have to tell the truth. If they didn't, we were all doomed. Anton would lose his freedom. His parents would lose their son. And I would lose my job, my license, and my reputation.

The next morning as I prepared for court, I reminded

myself of everything I had learned from Vera and Mihai. *Keep your head up and look straight at the prosecutor as he presents his arguments. Do not let him think he is intimidating you. When it is your turn, speak slowly and clearly, and always maintain eye contact with the judge.*

By the time I arrived in the courtroom, Anton was already seated at the inmates' box, and his parents were seated in the front row of the gallery. They all looked nervous. Inside, my stomach was in knots, but I did my best to project confidence, both for my client's sake and my own. Before I could speak with Anton or his parents, the judge entered. I recognized him immediately as Michael Token, the judge who had performed my swearing-in ceremony. Clearly, he recognized me too.

"I am sorry, but kids are not allowed in the courtroom," he said sternly, looking directly at me. Then he smiled and added, "You look so young!"

I was furious. This was not how I wanted to begin. I hadn't even spoken yet, and already I was not being taken seriously. I could feel the heat rising in my throat.

Don't let him get to you, I told myself. *You are prepared. You are confident. Just make your case.* Taking a cue from Vera, I stood as straight and tall as I could, took a deep breath, smiled politely, and launched into my opening statement.

"Your Honor, my client, Anton Sasu, is not guilty of purposefully burning a government document—in his case, his student Communist Party ID card. He did not intend to make a statement against the Communist Party as the prosecution has accused. Nor does he deserve to spend ten years in prison. He simply burned an old pair of school pants, unaware that his ID card was in the pocket. The card was burned purely by accident."

The courtroom was so quiet I could hear my heart pounding in my chest. I took a deep breath before making my next statement. It would be the most important comment of my entire career thus far—and possibly the most dangerous.

"Your Honor, both my client and his parents have informed me that they were forced into giving incriminating testimony at the police station—without an attorney present." The judge's gaze hardened, and I sensed movement from the prosecutor's desk off to my right.

"In light of this, Your Honor," I continued. "I would like to request that my client *and* his parents be allowed to testify today here."

Our eyes locked, and for a moment, I feared he would be able to see my heart pounding through my jacket. He leaned back in his chair, held my gaze for a few seconds more, and then quietly said, "I will allow that."

I breathed a sigh of relief. The first hurdle was cleared. Anton and his parents would be allowed to tell their stories. The question now was, which stories would they tell?

Anton took the stand first, and to my delight, he admitted that he had been coerced by the police into changing his testimony. Moments later, Anton's parents echoed their son's admission.

Yes! Though I maintained a professional demeanor, inside

I was practically giddy. Granted, we still had a long way to go, but at least my client and his parents were given the opportunity to tell the truth—and did! That, in and of itself, was an enormous victory.

Emboldened, I made one final request. "Your Honor, I request that my client be released during this trial so that he may continue his second year of school. He is an exceptional student, and I would like him to be able to continue his studies."

"I'll allow that," he replied. I heard Anton release a deep sigh of relief, and though I could not see her, I could have sworn I heard his mother gasp with joy.

The next court date was set for two months out. As the Sasus left the courtroom, they expressed their deepest gratitude for my help. I felt wonderful. My first court day had been a resounding success—except for one small thing.

"Please make me look older," I said, settling into the chair to have my hair cut.

My hairdresser laughed. "Oh, sweetie, it's your genetics. You should be glad. One day you will *want* to look younger."

"Maybe so, but not now," I said. Then I told her the judge's joke.

"Oh, it was just a joke," she said. "Are you sure you want me to cut all of this long, beautiful red hair? I can't put it back tomorrow if you change your mind, you know."

My look answered her question.

"Okay. I'll cut it short," she said, taking the comb and scissors in her hands. "How short do you want me to go?"

I showed her a picture in a magazine that I had picked up on my way home from court that afternoon. It was a chin-length bob style. Very simple and very professional looking. "Like this."

"Okay. If you're sure," she said as she quietly began cutting off eight-inch lengths of hair.

I don't know if I looked any older when she was finished, but I never heard another joke like the one I'd heard from Judge Token that day. That was good enough for me.

At home, my family loved my new hairstyle.

"You got a haircut!" squealed the girls, hugging me. "It looks so pretty!"

"This is sudden," Radu said. "What made you decide to do this?"

I told him what happened in court that day, and he laughed.

"You look like an Italian lady now!" He smiled, running his fingers through my shortened tresses.

"Mommy looks Italian! Mommy looks Italian!" The girls giggled.

"Enough, all of you!" I said, heading into the kitchen to start dinner and hoping that—at the very least—I looked like an *older* Italian lady.

*

Two months later, Anton's trial resumed, and after several weeks of intense arguing, I was able to convince the judge to reduce Anton's ten-year prison sentence down to two years of community service. He was also required to attend mandatory weekly rehabilitation and reeducation meetings to prove his continued allegiance to the Communist Party.

Though on the surface it seemed like a victory both for Anton and for me, the fact that he was found guilty and punished at all bothered me greatly. But the injustice did not end there.

A year later, Anton's mother came to see me about Anton's younger brother, who had also gotten into trouble with the government. She was so frail and ashen, I barely recognized her. She told me that since Anton's trial, her husband had been repeatedly harassed and interrogated by the police—for no apparent reason. Then one day during a particularly hostile interrogation, he suffered a heart attack and died. Shortly thereafter, Anton—completely defeated and discouraged by the reeducation process—hanged himself.

"I don't know what to do," she wailed in my office. "My children are terrified. The police keep coming to our house. They have already taken my husband and my oldest son, and now my other son is in trouble. I just . . . I just . . ." And then she fainted dead away.

Frantic, I called an ambulance, and the medics took her away. That evening I called all the hospitals in town, but not one of them had any record of her. She had simply disappeared. When I called to check on her children, I found that they had vanished too.

I wish I could say that Anton's family was the exception.

But in the years that followed, I met countless innocent people who were broken by the Communist regime or who disappeared following minor criticisms of or infractions against the government. I worked tirelessly to defend them and to fight for justice, but I was only one woman.

What I failed to realize was that the harder I fought, the more I became a target myself.

CHAPTER 9

Man can certainly keep on lying . . . ; but he cannot make truth falsehood. He can certainly rebel . . . ; but he can accomplish nothing which abolishes the choice of God.

—KARL BARTH

"I DON'T WANT TO BE an attorney anymore," I announced, walking into my office.

My secretary, Miruna, looked up from her desk.

"I became an attorney to find the truth," I continued, "and I'm not even sure the truth exists anymore." It had been a long week, and I was exhausted.

"Welcome to the real world," Miruna responded flatly, holding out a file folder. "Nestor Martin is waiting for you in your office."

I took the folder and entered my office to find Nestor Martin sitting peacefully in a chair with a contented smile on his face. "Good morning, Mrs. Prodan," he said, rising to meet me. "I wanted to talk to you about a few updates in my case."

Nestor's parents owned a house and some land in a rural area just north of the city of Ploieşti. The Communist government had confiscated the land when they took power, but due to increasing international pressure, they had been forced to return the property to the original families. Unfortunately, it was a slow and costly process, riddled with ever-changing fees and procedures, and since Nestor's parents were older, he was handling all the legalities.

As Nestor spoke, I found my thoughts drifting. I had spent my entire life searching for answers—first with my family, then in law school, and now as an attorney—but no matter how hard I tried, the truth always seemed to elude me. All I ever seemed to find were lies, injustice, fear, uncertainty, and defeat. And now I was feeling hopeless in my search. Life made no sense without something to believe in, and I had grown weary of searching only to come up empty time and time again.

Nestor continued speaking and placing new documents in front of me, but I didn't hear a word he said. I had been meeting with Nestor for months now, going over his parents' files. It was tiresome, tedious work with no end in sight, yet Nestor never seemed to get discouraged. He always had a smile on his face and a sense of contentment unlike anything I had ever seen. It was as though he were oblivious to all the misery that surrounded him every day. He appeared to radiate joy and peace. Frankly, it troubled me.

"I wish I had what you have in your life," I said absently.

"Sorry?" he said, glancing up at me.

"I wish I had your sense of peace and happiness."

He paused for a moment.

"Do you go to church?" he asked.

"Yes," I replied. "On Christmas and Easter. Why?"

"Would you like to come with me to *my* church this Sunday?"

I stared at him. *What does church have to do with anything?*

"I can pick you and your family up, and we can go together if you'd like."

He was persistent. I'd give him that.

"That's okay," I said. "I have a car."

Nestor wrote the name and the address of his church on a slip of paper for me.

"The service begins at nine," he said, handing me the paper.

I dropped it into my purse and tried to focus on his case, but my mind continued to wander.

I want Nestor's peace, his optimistic outlook on life, his sense of confidence even in the worst circumstances. If all of that comes from his church, then I will go and visit.

That next Sunday morning, my girls and I went to Nestor's church on the other side of Bucharest. As promised, Nestor was there waiting for us, smiling as always.

"I'm so glad you came," he said. "And who have we here?"

"These are my daughters, Anca and Andreea," I said, nudging the girls to shake Nestor's hand.

"So nice to meet you both," he said sweetly. "Will your husband be joining us as well?"

"No. I'm afraid he had some business to attend to in Ploieşti this morning," I responded.

Nestor laughed. "Ah. I hope he's not trying to get land back from the government, or he will be there awhile! Come inside. The service will be starting soon."

As we walked inside, I noticed how different it was from any church I'd ever visited. No icons of saints on the walls, no statues. The walls were plain white. Rows of chairs were separated by an aisle covered with old brown carpet. The men stayed on the left and the women and children on the right.

As we made our way toward the front of the church, the choir started singing. I didn't recognize the song, but I heard the words "sinner, come home." I wasn't sure what "sinner" meant, but everyone we passed smiled and nodded, and I felt very welcome.

As soon as the choir finished the song, the pastor approached the pulpit, opened the Bible, and read, "'I am the way and the truth and the life. No one comes to the Father except through me'—John 14:6."

Did I hear right? Someone was claiming to be "the truth"? The woman next to me handed me a Bible opened to John 14:6. I read the verse myself and then listened carefully. As the pastor continued to describe the truth of Jesus Christ, I felt as though he were speaking directly to me, that the Bible verses he was sharing were written specifically for me. *Could it really be this simple?* I thought. I looked across the aisle and found Nestor. He smiled and nodded at me and then gently patted his Bible as if to say, "Now do you understand?"

I did. Without realizing it, I was beaming back at him. For the first time in my life, everything made sense. I had spent years searching for the truth, but I had been looking in the wrong places—law school, the government, the justice system—when the answer was here all along. I suddenly realized that the truth was not something that came from law books, but from God himself: the Creator of the universe— my Creator; the source of all life, peace, and happiness.

When the pastor asked if anyone wanted to accept Christ as Lord and Savior, I accepted his invitation. It was the culmination of a lifelong search that went back as far as I could remember. I could barely contain my excitement. *Oh, I wish Radu were here,* I thought.

After the service was over, the pastor invited my girls and me into his office to talk. A few of the other church members joined us as well. We spoke for almost an hour, and before we left, they had arranged for the girls and me to begin a rigorous six-month Bible study program. They also gave us a Bible—and with it, a warning.

"You do realize," the pastor cautioned, "that the Romanian government can arrest you for having a Bible in your home."

I was vaguely aware of this fact, but I had never really given it much thought—until now.

"The government considers the Bible's teachings to be contrary to the Communist Party rules that require us to worship our president," he continued. "The government will not confiscate the Bible from our church, because they want to give the appearance to the West that Romania respects the freedom of religion. That is also why they permit our church to remain open." Then he leaned in slightly and lowered his voice to a whisper. "In time, you will discover that there are government spies within our church, as well as in others. You will learn to spot them soon enough." This did not surprise me at all. One of my earliest memories was the run-in I'd had just before Easter Sunday with the *Securitate* at my local church. Being placed on a list of "church people" had terrified me back then. For some reason, though, I did not feel anywhere near as frightened now.

"Virginia, are you *sure* you want to have this Bible in your home?" the pastor asked.

"Yes," I responded. "I am sure."

"Welcome to the church," he said, handing me the small leather book.

I quickly slipped it into my purse. Even though it was a fraction of the size of most of my old schoolbooks, I knew there was more truth contained in its delicate pages than there was in a full library of law books. I couldn't wait to get home and start reading.

Finally, I thought, *I have found what I was looking for.*

*

Weekly Bible training classes were held at the church with the pastor and two other leaders. Because it was dangerous to have printed materials, we just talked. Every week, I came with a list of questions about God, the Bible, and how to live the Christian life. "How do I know God hears my prayers?" "What is God's will?" "Do I start reading the Bible from the beginning or from the New Testament?"

Other times they would ask *me* questions to see how I was doing with my studies. Over the course of several weeks, they taught me the basics of the Christian faith and what it means to be a child of God.

And sometimes, they taught me unexpected lessons. One day, for instance, I was waiting outside the pastor's office when a man I had never met before approached me.

"My name is Constantin. Are you here to see the pastor? I can tell him you're here."

"Thank you," I responded. "I'll wait."

Constantin stood next to me. For a while no one talked.

"I heard you accepted Christ last month," he finally said.

"Yes, I did."

"Being a Christian is special; we are children of God, the Creator of heaven," he continued. "But the Christian life is not necessarily easy."

I looked at him. I had no idea what he was talking about. I was happy to be a Christian. I had finally found the truth, and in my mind, that made everything much easier.

Then he continued. "I was the pastor of this church many years back, when the *Securitate* pointed their guns at us and demanded that we renounce Christ or go to jail and die. Then we heard the church doors lock behind us.

"'Choose your side now!' one of the officers screamed. 'If you are for Christ, move to the left, and we will take you to jail immediately. But if you want to become a Communist, move to the right, and we will give you paperwork to sign.'

"I watched in terror as many of my brothers and sisters betrayed Christ that day," he continued. "Fearing for their lives, they moved to the right and signed the papers. A few of us, including myself, were taken. I spent five years in jail. After I was released, I was allowed to have a job again, but only as a janitor."

He looked at the ground, and his voice was barely audible. "Some of the others who were jailed with me didn't survive. Two of my brothers in Christ died in that jail from beatings and starvation." He paused for a moment before continuing.

"Nastase Albu was appointed as the new pastor by the government. We all suspected him of working with the *Securitate*. Because of him, many members of our church were arrested, and others left the church. Still other church members cooperated with the *Securitate* and served as spies. Those they did not like were eventually jailed or killed.

"Albu eventually moved on, and today, many of us have once again returned to this church." He looked up at me. "As a member of this church, how would you respond if you were asked to make that choice? Would you remain with Christ or become a Communist? Would you judge or forgive your brothers and sisters if they betrayed Christ? Virginia," he concluded, "how would you prepare yourself for a day like that?"

He stared me straight in the eye.

Surely that was a long time ago, I reasoned to myself. *That was a different time. Something like that could never happen again—could it?*

I knew Constantin was waiting for my answers, not my questions.

How would *I prepare myself for a day like that?*

I didn't have an answer for him—or myself, for that matter.

I had come a long way since accepting Christ. But clearly, I still had a long way to go.

*

Over the next several months, Constantin continued to challenge me to memorize Bible verses and to study God's Word. I studied not only Christ's life but also Paul's and Stephen's lives and their reactions to hard times and persecution. Both were full of faith and great examples to follow. I learned from them to pray for my enemies and to ask God to forgive my opponents not only for what they were doing to me but for what they did to themselves.

Despite all that he had been through, Constantin was a joyful and caring teacher who constantly encouraged me in my studies and rarely, if ever, talked about himself. I later learned that while he was in jail, his wife divorced him and married a Communist leader. He never remarried but instead dedicated his life to training others to become lay pastors.

I also got to know my pastor's family, as well as several other church members' families. Going to their homes, however, was an eye-opening experience. Their homes were simple and clean—far from the spacious apartment and custom furniture that Radu and I had. And yet, I was fascinated by their joy. Despite their meager possessions, they all looked so content, as though they were living not for material gain but for a higher purpose.

Even my pastor dressed mostly in worn and tattered clothing, which was a sharp contrast to my expensive wardrobe. But it wasn't just his clothing that seemed worn. His face was gaunt, and he looked old for his age and very tired. Yet when he spoke about God, he had an air of royalty about him.

While the girls and I enjoyed getting to know our new family in Christ, Radu had mixed feelings—about the new faith, the new church, and even our new friends. He struggled with all the changes in our lives—and with the changes in me. At times, his frustration took the form of criticism.

"This pastor makes so many grammar mistakes," he complained one day. It was true. The pastor did not have the best grammar, nor did he have the luxury of the advanced education that Radu and I had enjoyed. But his knowledge of the Bible was extraordinary. And in the end, I reasoned, isn't that what really mattered?

Later, I learned the reason for the pastor's lack of formal education. As soon as the Communist government took power, the number of Christian seminaries was reduced drastically. So, many pastors trained themselves and pastored as a second job. Rarely were they paid to serve the church. They were, however, always risking removal or persecution by the government.

"There is another Baptist church closer to our home," Radu continued. "Why don't we check out that one and see if you like it better?"

"But all of my friends are here," I countered.

"How can you like those boring people?" Radu asked. "All they do is talk about the Bible."

I didn't know how to respond. The fact that these people were so invested in God's Word is what drew me to them. Yet their fervor seemed to have the opposite effect on Radu.

It didn't help that Radu's mother was very vocal in her opposition to my new faith. On more than one occasion, she openly accused me of trying to get her son in trouble with the government by belonging to this church.

After a while, Radu found excuses not to go with the girls and me on Sundays. Instead, he spent his weekends hanging out with his friends at the horse track, betting on the races—and losing badly.

One day, I decided to confront him about it.

"Radu, we need to save money for a new car. If you continue betting on the horses, we'll never be able to afford one."

"That is my way of relaxing, Virginia," he countered. "And I have no intention of stopping."

"But we need to save money," I insisted.

Unexpectedly, Radu picked up a beautiful china vase that

Cassandra had given us as a wedding gift and threw it to the floor.

"Stop telling me what to do!" he shouted. "You are starting to sound like my mother!"

It had been a long time since I had seen Radu lose his temper. But now it was back with a vengeance.

After he stormed out of the room, I picked up the broken pieces and threw them away. My pastor and Constantin had both told me that knowing the truth sometimes comes at a cost. I was beginning to wonder if my marriage was about to become the price I would pay.

CHAPTER 10

The world is a dangerous place to live;
not because of the people who are evil,
but because of the people who don't
do anything about it.

—ALBERT EINSTEIN

AFTER SIX MONTHS OF studying the Bible, I was baptized, and almost immediately, churches and Christians who were being persecuted by the government began contacting me for help. And they needed it. Ceaușescu was a clever and deceitful leader. Early in his rule, he had led the Western powers to believe he was an anti-Soviet maverick by forcefully condemning a Soviet invasion of Czechoslovakia. But while he was publicly courting favor with America and Western Europe, internally he was building his own brutal and oppressive regime.

In an attempt to secure most-favored-nation status from America (greatly improving Romania's international trade rights), Ceauşescu promised to respect human and religious rights in Romania, to welcome visiting Western missionaries, and to allow Western Bibles to be brought into Romania. In reality, however, he ruled with an iron fist, confiscating Bibles, threatening to demolish churches, and vehemently persecuting Christians. Some were fired from their workplaces because of their faith. Others were jailed. Some simply disappeared. Families were destroyed. Pastors were replaced by others more loyal to the *Securitate*. Churches were infiltrated and subdued.

Not long after I began defending churches and individual believers in the Romanian courts, Pastor Paul Negrut, a leader among Romanian Baptist pastors, came to my office in Bucharest along with his wife and a few members from Hope Baptist Church in the city of Arad. They had driven some distance to ask me to take their case.

"Please, everyone, come inside," I said, inviting them in. "I understand you all have come a long way to see me. What can I do for you?"

"Thank you, Virginia, for taking the time to meet with us."

As they settled into chairs, Pastor Negrut, who was clearly the leader of the group, began to introduce the rest of them.

"This is my wife, Delia," he said, gesturing to a diminutive woman to his left. "And these are members of the church I spoke with you about. Doru Popa is the pastor of Hope Baptist Church, and Natan, Marius, and George are deacons. We are here because Hope Baptist Church asked permission from the Arad city government to make repairs to our building and to expand. First we were told there is a waiting list, and we were forced to wait for a full year. Then we were told to renew our request and were once again put on a list, this time for the following year." The other members of the group shook their heads in exasperation.

"Our church building was in desperate need of repair," Pastor Popa explained. "So, we decided to continue to renew our request but to also quietly fix the building without the government's permission. Everything was done by our church members and with our own money, but somehow the city government found out and threatened to demolish our church." He handed me a file folder containing letters from the city council.

"We need your help," Pastor Negrut implored. "No other lawyer will take our case."

"Please help us," Pastor Popa interjected. "We don't want to lose our church."

I quickly skimmed one of the letters threatening demolition.

"Okay," I said. "I will represent you and your church."

The five of them breathed an audible sigh of relief and broke into enormous grins, and the pastor's wife looked as though she might cry.

"Thank you," Pastor Negrut said, taking my hand in gratitude. "Thank you so much."

"You're welcome," I said, setting the file aside. "I will prepare a request to the city to give you permission to fix and expand your building; they will have ten days to respond.

I will also file a lawsuit against the Arad city government, requesting that the judge allow you to make the necessary repairs according to the current law we have in the books. If we don't hear back from anyone within ten days, we will meet in Arad to discuss our next move."

When our discussion was over, Pastor Negrut and his wife asked to speak with me in private.

"I know that you have represented other churches," he said, "and I feel that I should warn you. The Communist government does not like what you are doing, and if you continue taking cases like ours, you may be in danger."

"What kind of danger?" I asked.

"People are being thrown in jail or 'disappearing' for contesting the will of Ceaușescu," he explained. "In some cases, their children or aging parents are being threatened or killed as well." He nodded toward the photos of my daughters on my desk.

"We just want to make sure that you are fully aware of the risks you are taking in helping us," Delia emphasized.

I considered their warning. I knew that what I was doing was risky and that it could put both me and my family in danger. But I also felt very strongly that this was exactly what God wanted me to do. The entire reason I had become an attorney was to discover and fight for the truth. Now that I had found the ultimate truth, I had no intention of backing down—no matter the cost. Several months ago, Constantin had asked me how I would respond to the government threatening my life because of my faith. I did not know how to respond then, but I knew for certain now.

"You are both very kind," I assured them. "I do understand the danger, and I promise you I have every intention of doing my job and defending your church."

"You are very brave," Delia said. "And for that, we are grateful."

After I walked them to the door, I sat back down behind my desk. The pastor's warning played on a loop inside my mind. *I could be arrested . . . imprisoned . . . I could be killed . . . My children could be harmed . . .*

I thought of my precious daughters, Anca and Andreea. What if something happened to them because of my work? *Why should these two innocent ones suffer because of their mother's convictions?*

I felt a panic attack coming on. I knew what the pastor had said was not an exaggeration. Almost everyone in Romania knew someone—a friend, a relative, a coworker—who had suffered at the hands of the *Securitate*. Almost everyone could conjure up the anguished face of *someone* whose wife, husband, son, father, mother, aunt, or cousin had been taken away, never to be seen again.

I vividly remember being awakened during a quiet summer evening by terrifying screams coming from the house across the street.

"Don't take my mom away! She doesn't know where my dad is or what he said or did."

I recognized his voice. It was Aurel, a seven-year-old neighbor.

Aurel's father, Ciprian Vultur, had been an attorney too.

His wife, Gabriela, had come to ask me if I had seen her husband that day. She'd heard that Ciprian had stopped at the grocery store to buy some milk on his way home from the office, and someone said they heard him complaining that the government's price of milk was too high. After Ciprian left the grocery store, he vanished.

When I looked out my bedroom window, I saw a black *Securitate* car parked in front of the Vulturs' house. The door was wide open, and four officers were dragging a woman through it. They were followed by a near-hysterical Aurel.

"Please let my mom go!" he screamed in fear.

Having forced Gabriela into the backseat, the doors slammed shut, and the car sped away, leaving Aurel crying and shouting in the street. "Stop! I want my mom!"

As soon as the *Securitate's* car was gone, a red car drove up, and Sandu Florion, Ciprian's brother-in-law, got out, put the sobbing child in the car, and drove away.

Weeks later, I heard rumors that Sandu was a *Securitate* informant. I suspected he had something to do with Ciprian's disappearance, and I feared for Gabriela and Aurel.

I feared for myself as well. What happened to Ciprian and his family could happen to anyone, and I knew it. All that was necessary was to say the wrong thing at the wrong time in front of the wrong people. And here I was, taking that government to court. I was standing before judges and prosecutors and arguing against the government's policy of condemning churches in order to build more edifices for the glory of Nicolae Ceaușescu and his "golden age" of

Communism. I was making myself an open target for all
the hostility and intimidation the regime could bring. And
the Ceaușescu government had proven time and time again
that it was ruthless in imposing its will. Human lives meant
nothing; obedience was all that mattered.

*What right do I have to endanger the people I love? Are my
efforts doomed to fail? For what reason am I exposing myself and
my family to such peril?*

As these thoughts stampeded through my mind, I realized
I was at war with myself. My heart wanted to do what was
right, to stand up for the Christians and churches against
the godless regime. I truly believed that God had called me
to the legal profession for this purpose. And yet, how could
I put my family at risk like this? Fear for my life and for the
lives of my children began to encircle me, to build a prison
wall around my heart, and to whisper defeat into my ears.

I began weeping bitterly as I cried out to God. I grabbed
the file for the church case from my desk and hugged it to
my chest, close to my heart. *I understand the outer battle,*
I told God. *I can face adversaries in the courtroom and even
the* Securitate. *But I cannot win this inner battle between my
own heart and mind. Lord, you have to win this victory for me.
Take away my fear and replace it with a peace that surpasses
all understanding. I need your peace, Lord. I need your victory.*

I went on to share each of my fears in detail. *What if I or
my children are killed? What if I am imprisoned, and I never
see my daughters again for the rest of my life? What if someone
else I care about is punished because of what I'm doing?* I poured

my heart out to God, and as I did, I began to feel that he was listening, that he was taking each of my cares in his loving hands and offering me comfort.

After a long time, I looked down at the file I was clasping and realized that it was wet. I had been weeping and praying for so long that the file was soaked with my tears. But at the same time, I realized that the crippling fear had faded. God had taken away the agonizing battle between my heart and mind and replaced it with a victory of spirit. He had swept away the lies and replaced them with the truth of his love.

Tucking the file folder into my briefcase, I collected myself and headed for home. I could not remember a time I so desperately wanted to hold my daughters. I truly believed that God would protect us—the question was, from what?

*

Several days after Pastor Negrut and Pastor Popa came to see me, I was visited by two young Christian men named Martin and Liviu. Bibles were scarce in Romania, so churches would share them. Martin and Liviu's job was to transport Bibles between churches in Bucharest and across the country. They had to do it secretly, because Ceaușescu had forbidden Bibles to be removed from the churches—even though officially no law prohibited it. Like many Christians in Romania, Martin and Liviu didn't have their own cars, so they used the bus to do their work.

The *Securitate* didn't need a warrant to search people or

their belongings at any time or place, so being in possession of Bibles in a public setting like a city bus was excessively dangerous. Martin and Liviu had to be creative when it came to meeting their contacts and establishing safe locations to do the Bible exchanges. Truth be told, few couriers had done it as successfully and as many times as these two.

Martin was a middle-aged, small-framed, and energetic man. His parents, Martha and John, were rich and influential during the capitalist regime before Communism conquered Romania. After the Communists came to power, Martha and John were among the first arrested. Their home, cars, and belongings were all confiscated, and they spent five years being tortured and violently interrogated in jail without benefit of trial. Eventually they died in jail. After his parents were taken away, Martin was placed in an orphanage. He was never allowed to visit his parents in jail or communicate with them. He spent his days and years alone in the orphanage, working long hours on meaningless jobs. Many mornings his pillow would be wet with tears. No one knew of his pain, however, because he kept his feelings to himself.

When he turned eighteen, Martin was released from the orphanage without any money, relatives, a place to stay, or any right to continue his education. His first job was in a restaurant in Bucharest washing dishes. He was a hard worker, trustworthy and teachable. People liked him, but because of his history, the people who helped him did so cautiously or secretly so as not to come under government scrutiny themselves.

Martin worked and slept in the restaurant for almost six months. If something was wrong or not working in the restaurant, he learned to fix it. Fixing electrical problems was his specialty. Soon it became his calling.

Martin never married, but his love for people was visible, and he was always joyful. Despite the fact that the government had taken everything away from him, he had a special place in his heart for Communist leaders and prayed for them constantly. He also loved children and worked hard to make sure they had Bibles and knew God's truth.

Martin's colleague, Liviu, was a young and energetic Christian. Bucharest was not his hometown, but he learned to love it. He was born and lived in Bistriţa, a smaller town in the northern part of Romania. His father, Mark, was a devoted Communist, but his mother, Crina, hated Communism. Crina loved to teach Liviu about God even though it was against both her husband's will and the government's. She even kept a well-used Bible hidden in the attic.

One day Liviu's father returned home from work earlier than expected and found Liviu and Crina studying the Bible. He was furious. He considered Crina's actions both a personal and a governmental betrayal. He knew Crina must be punished and reported. He screamed at her, slapped her, pulled her hair, and then locked her in the barn. He also interrogated Liviu about the Bible and any other antigovernment actions his mother might have participated in.

The next morning, Liviu went to school. When he returned home, the house was full of relatives—many his dad's, some of them crying. They informed him that his mother had died suddenly of a heart attack, though his maternal grandmother later confided in Liviu that she suspected his dad had poisoned her as a punishment for her betrayal.

The funeral was held quickly, and few people attended. Not a month after the funeral, Liviu's dad married a much older Russian Communist named Natasha.

Liviu missed his mother and secretly hated Natasha. After about a year, Liviu ran away. He moved from one city to another, visiting and participating in underground church services. Many Christians offered him food or shelter. One day he met Claire, who had come from Bucharest to visit her grandmother for the summer. She worked at the church teaching children. Liviu helped her. They spent many hours together planning Bible lessons for kids. When summer ended, Claire returned to Bucharest, and they kept in touch via letters.

One day the church needed someone to transfer some Bibles to Bucharest, and Liviu volunteered. One of Claire's friends offered Liviu a place to stay so he and Claire could spend more time together. After a few months, they began to talk about marriage. The wedding was small but joyful, and afterward Liviu moved in with Claire and her parents.

A year into their marriage, Liviu learned that his stepmother had left his father for one of his father's superiors. Shortly thereafter, Liviu's father was burned to death in a suspicious house fire. In a small way, Liviu considered the fire justice for his mother.

One Sunday as I entered church, Martin and Liviu were there waiting for me. "We need to talk with you," Martin said urgently.

"Girls, go to your Sunday school class," I said to my daughters, ushering them away. "I'll come get you after church ends."

"Your pastor said we can use his office," Liviu said.

We walked in silence. After we entered the office, Liviu closed the door.

Martin began. "You know we transport Bibles. If something happens, we want to know you will represent us."

"Of course I will," I assured them. "But please be careful."

"We want to make sure you know what happened last time," Martin explained. "Liviu and I got on the bus, each carrying two suitcases full of Bibles. As soon as the bus drove away, I noticed two uniformed police officers sitting near the back, and my heart stopped for a second."

Liviu nodded as if reliving the experience. Martin continued. "Arrest, jail, even death flashed through my mind. I prayed like never before."

Liviu interrupted, "Me too! But I was determined to succeed. I thought about the joy that those Bibles and books would bring to so many kids!"

Martin got even more serious as he continued his friend's thought. "But what a disaster if they caught us. The entire shipment of materials would be destroyed."

Liviu pointed out what I'd been thinking: "But at that point, getting off the bus as soon as possible wouldn't have looked right." Liviu rubbed his temples. "At each bus stop, I hoped the policemen would leave. But no luck at all. They were both still there, watching. I kept asking myself, *Do they know something? Do they suspect something?*

"I felt my face turn hot, as the old passenger beside me kindly touched my knee and softly asked, 'Are you okay?' I realized I had to keep cool," he continued. "This was no time to panic."

"More people exited than entered at the next stop," Martin said. "The two policemen continued watching everyone."

"The next stop was mine," said Liviu. "So I picked up my luggage and stood calmly at the door. As the door opened, two other policemen were standing there, ready to come inside. One of them grabbed one of my suitcases and moved it to the pavement. I thought for sure they were going to look inside. But then they just got on the bus, and before I knew it, they were gone."

"We feel like we are closely watched," said Martin. "And we have another job this afternoon."

"We expect fewer policemen will be on the bus because it is Sunday," Liviu added. "But still . . ."

"Can someone else do this job for you for a while?" I asked.

"No," Martin replied. "We asked, but everyone is scared."

"We're fairly certain we will be okay, but we wanted to speak with you just in case," said Liviu.

Unfortunately, things did not go as Martin and Liviu had hoped. That afternoon, shortly after he completed his Bible exchange, Martin was arrested. Later that evening, Liviu was arrested too.

The next day, Martin and Liviu's pastor called my office to request an urgent appointment. He told me that both Martin and Liviu had been thrown in jail, and he worried that the government would soon discover the others who had been involved in the exchange. He gave me the little information he had as well as the name of the place where they were likely being held.

I called several police stations, but of course nobody knew anything. So, equipped with all the information the pastor had provided and the legal documents that indicated I represented Martin and Liviu, I set off for the police station where they were most likely to be held. I knew I needed to move quickly, or the police would try to force a false confession out of them as they had done with Anton and his parents—and countless others.

Once I arrived at the police station, I approached the clerk's window. "I am the attorney representing Martin and Liviu," I said.

The clerk looked at me and checked my documents. "They are not here. They were transferred to Station Two."

I rushed over there as quickly as I could. When I arrived, one policeman was posted at the door, and there was another one guarding the clerk's window. They recognized me instantly, as I represented several other people they had arrested in the past.

"I represent Martin and Liviu," I said, showing them my documents. The clerk took his time looking them over, then left the room. Finally, after twenty minutes, he returned. "They are not here. Station One has them."

"Are you sure?" I asked. "I just came from there. They sent me here."

"I know which criminals we are holding, and they are not here," he barked. "Now if you don't mind . . ." he said, looking over my shoulder to the next person in line.

As I walked back to the first station, Martin's father and his uncle joined me.

"What's the situation?" they asked.

"Just the normal dirty tricks," I said. "They're sending me from one station to another. Don't worry. I've done this before," I assured them.

When I got back to the first clerk's window, she acted busy, rifling through papers and refusing to make eye contact. I waited patiently for a few minutes, then I cleared my throat to get her attention.

"I would like to see Martin and Liviu immediately," I demanded. "I am their attorney."

She just stared at me blankly. Then the phone rang, and ignoring me, she picked it up and talked for almost fifteen minutes. When she finished, she left the room without saying a word. After several more minutes, she returned and said, "Officer Radulescu will be with you shortly. Please wait in the next room."

I walked into the room reserved for attorneys visiting clients and waited. In less than ten minutes, Officer Radulescu came in.

"Good to see you again, Mrs. Prodan." He shook my hand. "You've got quite the difficult job what with all of these criminals you represent." His self-confidence seeped through his words. "You are lucky. We did not have time to record Martin's or Liviu's interrogations, and there have been no confessions so far. But I know we will have their admissions soon." He looked directly into my eyes. "You can make our work harder," he said sternly, "but if you do, we can make your life a living hell. You know that, don't you?" I could almost smell his condescension. "So do yourself a favor and try to cooperate with us on this one, like your colleagues do."

With that, Officer Radulescu opened a door, and we walked into a small room without windows. In the middle of the floor sat a small wooden bench for the accused and two chairs, one for me and one for Officer Radulescu. One corner of the room held a floor lamp directed at the bench. The room was depressing, stuffy, and pungent with strange odors. There was no place to put my briefcase or my documents. I stood there, my eyes searching the room for hidden microphones.

The door opened, and a young officer shoved Martin, wearing a prisoner's uniform, into the room. The officer shoved him a second time, looking proudly at Officer Radulescu.

"Here is the criminal you asked for." He saluted Officer Radulescu, turned like a marionette, and left the room.

I approached Martin and tried to shake his hand, but he was handcuffed. "There is no reason to have him handcuffed," I said.

Officer Radulescu turned Martin around to free his hands. "But if he doesn't cooperate, I will put them back on."

"What part of the police procedure allows you to do that?" I asked Radulescu. "Martin has a constitutional right to talk freely, not handcuffed, with his attorney."

"Constitutional rights!" Radulescu let out a sinister laugh. "We are the constitution here."

"You know that is not right!" I turned my attention to my client. "Please sit down, Martin."

I sat on the chair provided for me, opened my briefcase, and took my documents and pen. Then, closing the briefcase, I set it on my lap to use as a desktop.

"Please tell me your part of the story," I said.

"We have his part of the story," Radulescu interrupted. "Liviu admitted guilt and is cooperating with us. My colleagues are interrogating him now."

"Where were you when the police arrested you?" I asked Martin, ignoring the officer's interruption.

"Remember you are in our custody!" Officer Radulescu warned him.

I was beginning to feel exasperated. "Officer Radulescu, may I interview my client, please?"

"I was walking from Agape Baptist Church to the Maranatha Baptist Church to bring them Bibles for their Vacation Bible School," Martin replied.

"Liar!" Radulescu stood up and screamed. "Those Bibles are clandestine items from the West! I can charge you with being a spy for America."

"Officer Radulescu, please," I said sternly. "You have made your statement. Now it is my turn."

"Is this the way Baptist churches help each other during Vacation Bible School?" I asked.

"Yes," Martin replied. "We had done this exchange before, both last year and the year before. You can check with the pastors."

Martin was bruised and looked tired. Yet his eyes were still full of light.

"Is this your first time being arrested?" I asked.

"Yes," he replied.

After forty-five minutes, Radulescu decided that Martin's time with his attorney was over. I couldn't complain, as Radulescu was allowed by law to establish that.

I said good-bye and hugged Martin as Officer Radulescu handcuffed him. The door opened and the young mario-nette officer walked into the room and pushed Martin out the door.

"Well, clearly Martin is guilty," said Radulescu. "He will confess soon, and I am confident that Liviu will cooperate with us. We will make sure of that. There is nothing you can do about it."

I looked directly into his eyes and reached out to shake his hand. "Thank you for your time, Officer."

As I walked away, I heard him laughing behind me, declaring, "We are in charge here."

They may have thought that, but Martin's faith proved them wrong. Even after being brutally tortured, Martin refused to betray Christ. During my later visits, the guards complained to me that Martin and Liviu spoke only about Christ and his love for people and for the guards in particular. Even after long interrogations, Liviu sang in his cell, and Martin prayed for the guards by name.

"You cannot take this Christ from them," one guard said, puzzled. "I think they have both gone crazy!"

I was encouraged by Martin's faith but concerned about his health. *Freedom is so precious,* I thought.

After my first meeting with Martin, his father and uncle approached me outside the jail. "Is Martin alive?"

"Yes. He is alive. He needs our prayers more than anything."

"I have the name of two people who were present when Martin was arrested," Martin's father said. "Also, here is Liviu's wife's phone number. She would like to talk with you."

"Thank you," I said, taking the number. "I can stop by her apartment and talk with her on my way home tomorrow."

After we parted ways, I went straight to my office. I made several phone calls, including one to the prosecutor's office to find out the charge lodged against Martin and the name of the prosecutor handling the case. It turned out that Dorian Popa, one of my law-school classmates, was in charge of Martin's case.

Dorian was a devoted prosecutor eager to earn the government's trust and a promotion. His wife and I had had the same doctor when we were pregnant. She delivered their baby boy the same day that I delivered our second daughter,

Andreea, and our children had shared many playdates over the past few years.

But that was before I accepted Christ and started defending churches and other Christians. Since then, Dorian had been avoiding me, and our kids' playtimes together began to be delayed, rescheduled, and finally canceled. Soon we just stopped interacting altogether.

This appointment with Dorian would be my first professional contact with him. I wondered if Dorian would try Martin and Liviu together. I was convinced he was the one who provided the "admission testimony" for Liviu that Officer Radulescu had mentioned repeatedly.

Walking toward Dorian's office, my hope of having a friendly collaboration was low, but my faith in God was never stronger. I knocked, and a middle-aged blonde with blue eyes opened the door.

"Hello. I am here to see Dorian Popa," I said.

"Yes, he is waiting for you, Mrs. Prodan," she responded. "Please have a seat. I will tell him you're here."

I sat on a chair in the reception area. A huge picture of Dictator Ceauşescu hung on the wall, flanked by smaller pictures of Lenin and Marx. On the bookshelf were all the books and articles that Ceauşescu or his wife had written. And on the receptionist's desk were a small Romanian flag and pictures of the dictator with Fidel Castro, Mao Zedong, and other prominent Communist leaders.

After several minutes, the door opened, Dorian's secretary invited me in, and I walked into a big, bright office. Dorian's desk was custom made of dark cherrywood. He looked very powerful sitting in his executive chair, intently writing something on a legal pad.

"Sit down," he said without looking at me. Then the phone rang, and he picked it up and talked for almost ten minutes without making eye contact with me.

I put my briefcase on the small table in front of me and took a few documents from it. Finally he hung up and said, "How can you defend criminals like Martin and Liviu? They are nothing but spies for capitalists. I can charge them with treason, you know. Receiving goods from capitalists! Or promoting capitalism."

Before I could even formulate a response, he continued. "And you! How can you defend them the way you do? Even if they hired you, you must remain loyal to our leader. You are a Romanian attorney!" He slammed his fist against his desk and glared at me.

"The police are still working on Martin and Liviu, you know," Dorian continued. "We will have a confession anytime now. I have already ordered that the spies be transferred to prison once we do, and I will make sure they die there."

I was momentarily speechless.

"All your life, you were taught that we don't need Bibles," he went on. "We have our leader's directions. *He* is our god! You are not helping by going to the police station and encouraging your criminal clients not to confess. I would hate to see you end up in jail for that." His face was red as he slammed his fist down on his desk again. "I am ashamed of you!"

"What are you talking about, Dorian?" I asked incredulously.

"Martin and Liviu had two pieces of luggage filled with Bibles and Christian books with them when they were arrested," he said.

"Show me the Romanian law against it," I countered. He said nothing. "I can show you the law that protects them," I continued. I was surprised by my calm demeanor, contrasted with his violent anger.

Finally he spoke. "Our leader's direction trumps the law."

I couldn't believe I'd heard him say that. I looked straight at him. His eyes were blazing and full of hate. "May I see the file, please?" I asked calmly.

He picked up the phone. "Angela, please bring me Martin and Liviu's file."

The door opened, and Angela came in with the file.

"Please stay here and watch Mrs. Prodan," Dorian instructed Angela. "I have to leave." He turned his glare toward me. "If you have any questions, we can set up another meeting." And with that, he stomped out of the room.

I took the file and studied it, trying to forget everything Dorian had said. Angela was there supervising me. She was hovering so close, I could hear her breathing.

After I finished looking through the file, I placed it back on Dorian's desk. "I'm done," I told her.

"Good," she responded, gesturing toward the door. "Remember, if you have any questions, call to set up another appointment. However," she added, "it might be a while. We have been very busy lately. Dorian is an extremely successful prosecutor, you know."

"Thank you," I said, leaving without further comment.

Back in my office, I reviewed my notes. I was concerned but not afraid. There was no doubt Dorian now considered me an enemy. I had to prepare a strong defense against him. I knew that using the Romanian law protecting Martin and Liviu would be dangerous for me, but it was the only chance my clients had. More importantly, it was the right thing to do. After all, I reminded myself, *freedom is precious.*

After months of visiting Martin and Liviu in jail, collecting evidence, and interviewing witnesses, we finally got our day in court. I also spoke with their parents and Liviu's wife one more time before the trial. All of them had agreed to testify, risking their own freedom in the process. Of course, the prosecution used ambush tactics, not sharing their witness information until they were called to testify before the judge.

The courthouse was a tall, impressive building constructed during the capitalist era. It had strong, classic architecture. Symbols of justice were engraved at each corner, and each entrance featured impressive arches and statues. The building had four aboveground levels for offices and courtrooms— the places where justice should have been done but where punishment would be imposed on all enemies of the state. There were also two underground levels. Rumor had it that the underground went even deeper, but only *Securitate* had access to those levels. Rumor also had it that many dissidents or lovers of capitalism disappeared and died down there.

My clients' families went directly to the small courtroom where Martin and Liviu's case would be handled to make sure they would have a place to sit. Few seats were available, and many times the police refused relatives access.

As I entered the south entrance, I went down a few steps and walked down a long hall. Some people were waiting in line near the docket list; others spoke with their attorneys. Past the small courtrooms, a grand rotunda opened. On the right of the rotunda was a large room for attorneys. A small waiting room was nearby for clients. Many attorneys had coffee, lunch, or negotiation meetings there with their opponents. The air was redolent of the Western cigars that many attorneys smoked. I used the attorneys' room only to meet with my opponents, to finalize something before a trial, or to meet new clients from outside Bucharest. Before I had my girls, I used to have breakfast or coffee meetings there with law-school classmates. Now the smoke was so thick that I decided to avoid it. I was not a smoker, and when I got home in the evenings, I had to hang my suit outside because of the putrid smell that penetrated it.

As I walked toward the courtroom, my heart raced, but my mind rested on God. I reminded myself, *This is his battle, and I am his tool.* My heart relaxed, and I confidently walked up the middle aisle toward the attorneys' tables. Behind the judge's seat was a big picture of our leader and the Romanian flag. To his left was the prosecutor's desk, and seated at it was Dorian. He looked stressed but in control.

Just then the door opened, and Martin and Liviu were

ushered in. They were dressed in orange jail uniforms, and their hands were cuffed behind their backs.

"Who represents these men?" the judge asked.

"I do, Your Honor," I replied.

"Counselor, what are the charges against these men?" he asked, looking at Dorian.

Dorian stood, and in a strong, clear, confident voice explained the charges against Martin and Liviu.

"The defendants are accused of carrying weapons with the intent to do harm and to defy the Romanian government," he began. "In Romania, if you carry a weapon, you need a permit. The Bible, Your Honor, is a weapon, and as such, you have to have a permit to carry it. Martin and Liviu did not have a permit, and they carried *many* Bibles. The punishment for such a crime is twenty-five years in prison, and we are asking for the maximum sentence."

After he sat down, it was my turn.

"Your Honor," I began. "My clients, Martin and Liviu, had two pieces of luggage filled with Bibles and other Christian books with them when they were arrested; that is true. They were transferring those Bibles and Christian books from one Baptist church to another for use in Vacation Bible School. According to Law 217, we have the right not only to have Bibles but to share those Bibles with other churches."

I approached the judge with a file. "Your Honor, here is a copy of this law." Then I approached Dorian. "And Mr. Prosecutor, here is a copy for you."

Disbelief and anger gleamed in their eyes. Law 217 was

adopted by the capitalist regime long before Communism came to Romania, but Ceaușescu never rescinded it, because he was concerned about proving to the West that he was tolerant. In reality, though, he threatened anyone who dared use the law. Most attorneys had forgotten it even existed.

"Yes, in Romania, if you carry a weapon, you need a permit," I continued. "Just as the prosecutor said. But he forgot that private citizens cannot carry weapons—only *Securitate* officers and members of the Grand National Assembly. And the Bible is not a weapon. Therefore, I argue that my clients are *not* guilty, and I would ask that the court release them immediately."

After hearing the testimonies of Martin's and Liviu's relatives and the pastors of both churches, the judge announced that he would have a decision within a month. I left the courtroom feeling cautiously optimistic. I knew that the law was on our side, but I also knew how little that meant for those who dared speak out against the government. Still, I had done my best. Now Martin's and Liviu's fates were in God's hands.

Later that night, while listening to the Voice of America on the radio, I heard a detailed discussion about the case. The reporter praised my courageous determination to use an old, "forbidden" Romanian law to free my clients.

I knew the government monitored my daily life, but I wondered how the Voice of America had gotten that information. After all, they were not allowed to enter Romania, much less a Romanian courtroom. Regardless, I knew that now my life was in even more danger.

Just then, one of my girls called to me.

"What's wrong, Andreea?" I asked, sitting down on the edge of her bed. "Did you have a bad dream?"

"Yes," she said, her voice trembling. "I dreamed that you were arrested."

"Oh, don't you worry about that," I said. "I'm right here." I gave her a big hug. "Now go back to bed." I tucked the blanket over her and gently rubbed her back until she fell asleep.

Lying in bed that night, I thought about the possibility of being arrested. *It could happen,* I thought. I wasn't behind bars, but I suddenly felt as lonely and frightened as I imagined Martin and Liviu must have felt that night.

Please God, I prayed, *watch over Martin and Liviu. Watch over all of us.*

A month later, the judge pronounced his decision. He agreed with me that Martin and Liviu were just transporting Bibles between churches for Vacation Bible School and that their activity was protected by Law 217, and he ordered that Martin and Liviu be released immediately from jail.

As I read the judge's decision, I was overwhelmed, and I prayed the words of Psalm 66:3. *O Lord, "How awesome are your deeds! So great is your power that your enemies cringe before you."*

I rushed to the jail just as my clients were released. Tired, skinny, and dressed in wrinkled and moldy-smelling clothes but with light in their eyes, Martin and Liviu ran to me, and we embraced. Our joy was indescribable.

As soon as we got in my car, we sang together, "I have

decided to follow Jesus; no turning back; no turning back," as rivers of tears flowed down our cheeks. Our hearts were full of heavenly praises.

No turning back, indeed.

CHAPTER 11

The law of the LORD is perfect, refreshing the soul.
The statutes of the LORD are trustworthy, making
wise the simple. The precepts of the LORD are right,
giving joy to the heart. . . . The decrees of the LORD
are firm, and all of them are righteous.

—PSALM 19:7-9

As ELATED AS I WAS to see Martin and Liviu go free, deep down I knew they were only two of hundreds, possibly thousands, of Christians being persecuted by the government because of their faith. The very next day, in fact, I was due back in court to defend two Christians who had been thrown in jail for watching a film about Jesus Christ in their home and a doctor who was in danger of losing her medical license for sharing a Bible with one of her patients.

I grew up in Communist Romania, but at times like this, even *I* still had to ask myself, *How did we get here?*

My mind drifted back to childhood memories of Christmas. I will never forget the first year I was allowed to travel to Constanta with the rest of the family to receive "Christmas gifts" from the Communist Party.

"Really? I can go with Alina, Oana, and George to Dad's work?" I asked.

"Yes." Elena quickly brushed me off. "Make sure you have your uniform ready."

"Do we have to wear our school uniforms?"

"Yes, you do," she snapped back. "And only say yes or no. Nothing else. I will not have you embarrassing us all."

I went to sleep that night dreaming about traveling to Constanta, seeing where Stephen worked, and receiving a gift. I imagined there would be a room *full* of gifts. *Maybe I will even get to choose mine,* I thought.

The next morning, we walked to the bus. For the first time, I felt part of the family. I put on my gloves and my hood. The snow was still high, but the streets were cleaned. When the bus arrived, we all found seats, and I was lucky enough to get a window.

"Look how tall that building is!" I exclaimed, watching the giant skyscrapers whiz past.

"Be quiet!" Stephen said.

For the rest of the trip, I kept my thoughts to myself, which was a challenge, as literally everything was new and fascinating—the streets, the buses, the cities, the people.

After two hours, we pulled up in front of a large building. Stephen turned to me and said very sternly, "We are at the Communist Party headquarters where Santa's party will take place. Remember, only say yes or no, nothing more."

I glanced out the window. The building had an imposing entrance with large stairs and a tall, wide door.

"Is this where you work, Dad?" I asked. "There are no Christmas decorations around the entrance or on the door."

"No. Now be quiet." His face was red, and he had his finger pointed directly at me. Not a good sign. You would have thought I had killed someone.

We entered a large reception room decorated in red, the official color of Communism. We were taught in school that red symbolized the blood the Communists shed to save us from the horrors of capitalism so we could live in justice and equality under the new regime.

On each wall there was a big picture of our leader, flanked by Marx's and Lenin's pictures, and there was a Romanian flag in each corner. *Just like in school,* I thought. The ceiling was very high, and the chandeliers were beautiful. The windows were bordered with red draperies. It reminded me of the capitalist mansions Uncle Carol used to describe.

I walked to the left side of the room, where a small Christmas tree stood. Its decorations puzzled me—only some little pictures of soldiers who had died for us, a picture of our leader, and on top, a big, red Communist star with a yellow hammer and sickle. *I have never seen a Christmas tree decorated like this,* I thought, *with no angels and no silver Bethlehem stars.*

I looked around the room. All the children were dressed in school uniforms, and we all wore red scarves, the symbol of the Communist Pioneers. The parents were silent. Nobody exchanged a word. It felt like we were at a museum.

"Children, come here," a large man on the other side of the room barked. "It is time for you to sing."

My parents had told me we would sing Communist patriotic songs. I still hoped for at least one Christmas song.

I had always loved Christmas caroling. Adults did not go—celebrating Christ would be seen as acknowledging a power higher than Ceaușescu—but we children would venture out early in the morning while it was still dark, going only to trustworthy relatives' or friends' homes. We would knock two times on the window, and they would quickly open the door for us to come inside and sing. Sometimes they even sang with us. Our singing was always soft—so neighbors would not hear and report us to the *Securitate*—but joyful. When we finished, we would receive homemade cookies or candy, but we had to eat quickly.

"You make sure you are home before the sun rises," Elena would warn us. "And keep your faces covered as much as you can. Don't let the *Securitate* recognize you. If they stop you, let them have your cookies and run as fast as you can."

A strong clap woke me from my daydream.

"That was wonderful, children. Very patriotic! You will grow up to be good Communists. Now you can have some drinks and cookies." The man pointed toward a table bearing store-bought cookies in the shape of the Romanian flag or decorated with Communist symbols.

"Which one would you like?" a small woman with a heavy Russian accent asked. "You can have only one." After scanning the table, I picked one covered in plain red. It seemed the most Christmassy. It was stale, and the frosting was tasteless. I thought about homemade Christmas cookies—the aroma, the taste, and the love that came with them, especially the ones that came from the older relatives who would cry for joy when singing Christmas carols with us.

"Because you all sang so well, you will now have the honor of meeting the Communist Party leader of Constanta, Comrade Proplian!" the large man, who seemed to be in charge, said.

We quickly and silently formed a long line in front of Comrade Proplian as we were instructed. When I got to the front of the line, Comrade Proplian looked down at me. "Here, little girl. Pioneer Virginia, yes?" he asked, quickly conferring with the large man next to him, who nodded. "Santa Claus asked me to give you this gift," he said, handing me a doll. "It looks just like you—a future Communist leader!" he said. "You know Santa and the Communist Party love you. Do you like it?"

I took the doll. It looked like a teacher or an economist with a little red scarf on her neck—a Pioneer just like me. Comrade Proplian bent toward me. He had a full, fat face and was wearing a nice black suit with a patriotic tie, shiny shoes, and lots of cologne.

"Are you sure you like it?"

I felt Stephen's right hand shaking on my back. "Yes. Yes. Thank you." Then Stephen took me by my hand and pulled me toward his other side.

I looked at the doll. It looked stiff, like Communist leader

Olga, who came to our class every Friday at two o'clock to train us on how to become a good Communist leader like her. One time, one of my classmates whispered something to me, and Olga made us stand and hold our hands up during her entire presentation. The memory of the excruciating pain in my arms almost made me drop the doll. Then I heard Stephen say, "Thank you, Comrade. Long live the Communist Party!" He sounded like a soldier, and his face was red. I hugged my gift in fear.

On the bus ride home, the parents were all silent, and the children spoke only about their gifts. All the gifts had a Communist theme. The boys received Communist soldier toys or books about our "Beloved Leader"; the girls received red-scarfed dolls.

When we returned to school, our teacher required us to share in front of the class what our special "Santa" gift was and to write an essay about it and how thankful we were to receive it. We were reminded not to use the phrase "Christmas gift"—unless we wanted to be punished with an additional ten pages.

At recess that day, I heard two of my classmates talking.

"What gift did you receive from your parents?"

"My parents told me that Santa's gift was from them. They said *they* paid for it."

Our teacher must have heard them too, because after recess she said, "Raise your hand if your parents told you that Santa's gift was from them and not from our Beloved Leader." A few hands went up. I found out later that those parents were put on the black list and sent to Communist rehabilitation classes.

The next year, the Santa event at the Communist Party headquarters was different. From the bus station, we walked for almost an hour to the headquarters, and the gifts were distributed outside the back door through a small window. We had to wait in line for hours in the cold. At one point, people were pushing and cutting in line. It was a long, crowded, and unpleasant experience.

The comrade's gift for me that year was a small red book with pictures of our Communist leaders and of student Pioneers my age joyfully learning the Communist rules. For Stephen's sake, I pretended to like it.

By the time I was fourteen, I was too old to receive gifts, so I didn't go. Still, I was required—as was everyone my age at school—to express my gratitude for gifts I never received. The punishment for not doing so was failing the class.

Over the years, the official propaganda publicly replaced "Santa Claus" with Dictator Ceaușescu's name. And things got worse from there. Ceaușescu methodically created a godlike image for himself. It was just one of the many ways the Communist regime tried to destroy Romanians' belief in God and to replace Christ with Ceaușescu and the Bible with *The Communist Manifesto*. Television programs idealized Ceaușescu and his childhood, radio stations were required to play music written to glorify him, and bookstores replaced classics with books about our new all-knowing and all-powerful "god on earth." Even the Orthodox Church of

Romania supported this personality cult that was essentially worship of the dictator. Being disobedient resulted in either jail, death, or "disappearance." The guilt of one family member carried the punishment over to the entire family.

How the government knew the most secret information about a normal family, I had no idea as a child. Now that I was an adult, however, I understood all too plainly. After all, most of my clients were victims of *Securitate* spies. Sadly, even the underground church had its spies.

Two of my newest clients, Nina and Ovidiu Lungu, were members of an underground church in Bucharest. They lived in a blue-collar area loyal to the Communist government. They were not zealous Communists, but neither were they outspoken rebels. Though their Christian faith was strong, they avoided taking any church leadership roles for fear of being singled out. Just going to church was risky enough. Ovidiu's father, for example, was trained as an Orthodox priest under capitalism. Shortly after the Communists took power, he simply disappeared as he was walking from church to visit a sick member. As with many priests or pastors who disappeared during those years, nobody knew what happened to him. Not long afterward, his wife was evicted from her home, and the government confiscated all of their belongings.

Early in his tenure, the new Orthodox priest whom the government had supplied to replace Ovidiu's father proved to have no knowledge of or love for the Bible. Instead, his main interest was taking confessions from the church members.

Needless to say, people suspected him to be a spy. When they stopped making confessions, he would show up at their homes and wander around the house unbidden, looking into closets, rooms, and drawers, all in the name of blessing it. His visits often ended with him requesting payment for his blessing. It was the Communist way.

Many times, an underground church had only two families and no more than six or ten people, so a church meeting was more like a family gathering. Even so, the government considered it a threat.

It was too risky for these churches to keep a Bible or a hymnal. Even if it hadn't been risky, it was nearly impossible to obtain printed Christian materials in Romania during those years. Yet true believers committed dozens, even hundreds, of Bible verses and passages to memory. The Communists could confiscate printed materials, but they could not wipe the Word out of believers' hearts.

On occasion, though, new Bibles or books came secretly from the West. Later, the *JESUS* film came as well. And so the underground church grew. Each Bible, book, or movie was passed and shared among all the members, and the Word could neither be silenced nor snuffed out.

After a long wait, Nina and Ovidiu were secretly informed by a church friend, Tom, that they could pick up their copy of the *JESUS* film the following week. Tom worked in a small cigar store, so Ovidiu went to the store, ostensibly to buy some cigars, shampoo, and toothpaste. He paid, and Tom placed the video in the bag along with Ovidiu's purchases.

No one else was in the store at the time. Ovidiu then placed the brown bag in a dark shopping bag he carried with him and continued shopping at a few more stores, making sure he was not followed. Then he took the bus home. When his children went to their daily playdate with their cousins, he sent them with an invitation to come the next week to celebrate his birthday and watch the movie. He instructed them not to bring gifts, to avoid attracting the government's attention. The following week, four of Ovidiu's nieces and nephews joined the Lungus in their apartment. Twenty minutes into the movie, they heard a loud knock on the door.

"Are you expecting anyone else?" Nina asked Ovidiu.

Before Ovidiu could respond, a louder knock interrupted.

"Police! Open the door!"

The family members couldn't even move before the police punched through the door and invaded the home. Six policemen with guns handcuffed Nina and Ovidiu and unplugged the TV to confiscate it, while the children cried and pleaded for the adults' lives.

The officers began yelling at the children, "You need church? We will educate you on that! Ceauşescu is god, not that lunatic in your movie. We will teach you to be good Communists."

One of the officers then slapped and shoved Nina and Ovidiu all the way downstairs, pushing them into the walls. The officers forced the couple into the police car and disappeared into the night. The children ran back into the house crying, asking each other what to do next.

"I will call our uncle," one said, picking up the phone. "No dial tone. The phone has been cut off."

Another boy ran outside to the neighbors' house, hoping he could use their phone.

"Who is it?" the neighbor asked upon hearing the boy's frantic knocking.

"Andrei, from next door."

There was no answer from behind the door. Having witnessed the scene moments ago from their window, the neighbors had no intention of getting involved.

After a while, the two oldest boys decided they would walk the two hours to their uncle's home. He was a Christian and would help them. The others would stay overnight with the two girls (four and six years old) and twin toddlers.

"Turn off the light and look outside," whispered one of the boys. "See if we are being guarded by the police."

"I don't see anyone," replied another. "We have to go now. You take care of the girls and the babies," he said to the other boys. "We will be back tomorrow after school." The children hugged each other and prayed, and the older boys left the house. Cautiously, they walked outside the apartment. There was no sign of the police. Walking quickly along the dark streets, they looked right and left for policemen. None. In silent sorrow, they walked to their uncle's home. Exhausted, they knocked on the door.

"Who is it?" their uncle asked.

As soon as they responded, the door opened.

"What are you doing outside at this time of night?" the uncle inquired. "What's going on?"

From the hallway, the boys heard their aunt's voice, "Who is it at this hour? Was someone murdered or arrested?" Soon the entire family was up and in the hallway. The boys started crying. No one could understand them through their sobs.

Eventually, the uncle sent his own children back to sleep and took the two boys into the master bedroom with his wife. "Tell us everything."

"We were watching the *JESUS* film when the police came," one of the boys explained between sobs. "They broke down the door and arrested our parents. We don't know where they took them."

The uncle and aunt looked at each other. "You stay here for the night. I'll take you to school tomorrow," their uncle said.

In a soothing, motherly tone, their aunt added, "I'll make up a bed for you."

After the boys were asleep, their aunt and uncle set about devising a plan.

"We need to speak to our pastor and find someone to represent Nina and Ovidiu," he whispered to his wife. "Let's hope they're not charged with conspiracy or treason, like our niece was." He could see his wife's pained look even in the darkness, so he put on his best, most reassuring voice. "Go to sleep. God is still in control."

The morning came early for them—and for me, too, that day. I had forgotten to draw the blinds the night before, so the radiant sun had awakened me earlier than usual. I fixed breakfast, took a quick shower, and dressed for work. Radu was out of town on business, so I got the girls dressed and ready for school.

I thought about the day ahead. They say that faith can move mountains, and that was certainly true in my case. I had gone to bed crying and praying. I woke up praying and full of hope. Feeling God's power, I walked quickly to my office.

"Good morning," I said to my assistant as I passed her desk.

"Someone wants to talk with you." She handed me the phone.

"Hello. I got your number from Pastor Josef Stefanut. I need to see you this morning. It is an emergency."

Whenever someone got my number from a pastor, it was always an emergency.

"I can see you in an hour," I said.

An hour later, a tall man with white hair and brown eyes entered my office. I motioned for him to be seated. He sat and put his file on the table in front of him. "My relatives, Nina and Ovidiu Lungu, were arrested last night," he began. "I don't know why. They were watching the *JESUS* film, one of the new movies we got from our brothers in America. I myself watched it with five of my relatives at my home last week. The movie has circulated to several church members without incident."

"Okay," I said, grabbing a pen to take notes. "Let's go back to the movie's circulation during the weeks before their arrest."

He opened the file and took out a note. "I have tracked that with my pastor and some trustworthy brothers."

"Good," I said, taking the note. "Do you know if anything unusual occurred in the weeks or days before their arrest?"

He rubbed his eyes. "I am not aware of anything, but I can ask their children."

Children? My mother-instinct kicked in. "How old are the children? Where are they staying now? Do they go to school?" I asked.

"They are staying with me for now, and yes, I took them to school this morning."

I jotted a few things down on a legal pad and handed him the list. "Here are a few things I need from you. In the meantime, I will find out where they are being detained. You need to pay the attorney's fees for each one so I can represent them. Once I have those representation documents, I should be able to see them—or at least talk with the police or the prosecutor in charge."

He seemed to expect those instructions. "Our pastor and several members offered to help with a collection. My brother Anton will be here with money within an hour."

*

On the day of Ovidiu and Nina's trial, I had another client to defend as well. Some years earlier, a Pentecostal pastor in Bucharest who was also an aerospace engineer had been thrown in jail and sentenced to five years in prison for having a Bible in his home, teaching his children about Christ, and sharing his Bible with others. Now, years after his release, his family was once again in trouble with the government. This time it was his wife, Adina Cosma, a medical doctor, who was facing charges. She had visited a pregnant woman at her home and prescribed medication. When she visited again the next day, the patient was upset because the government pharmacy had refused to provide the medication. Adina tried to calm the woman down and offered to pray with her. Before she left, she pulled a Bible from her bag and gave it to her patient. At first, the patient said she was happy to have her own Bible, but later, she reported the doctor to the *Securitate*, hoping the government officials would provide her with the necessary medication in exchange.

The formal government charges against my client were possessing a Bible, transporting a Bible, and sharing the gospel. No Romanian laws prohibited any of those actions. But I knew too well that the government would continue making these kinds of charges if no one dared to confront them.

According to my client, the patient was too frightened to retract her testimony. The trial was set for that afternoon, and I was not sure if her patient would be courageous enough to tell the truth. So I was ready to once again use Law 217. As before, I had copies ready for both the judge and the prosecutor.

Under the Communist regime, the prosecutor was allowed to change the charges at any time, even before closing arguments. This method of trial by ambush was typically reserved for Christians or dissidents. For example, because the Bible my client had offered was printed in America, the government could charge her with smuggling foreign products into Romania, or even consider her a spy for America. Anything was possible. And as soon as they had taken her down, they would go after her husband. Still, Law 217 was my best and only hope.

I packed my files into my briefcase and started out for the courthouse. As I walked past my assistant's desk, I told her, "Please take all calls for me, and close the office if I am not back by five o'clock."

As soon as I left the building, I felt as though I was being followed. The steps behind me sounded like a man's. I walked slowly past stores with big windows, hoping to see the man's face. No luck. *Maybe it is just in my mind.* But I knew it wasn't. I could even hear his heavy breathing. I entered the next store and turned around, but no one was there. *Am I going crazy?*

I left the store praying for peace. I walked quickly and didn't hear the steps following me. I stopped at the stoplight and watched the cars driving in front of me. Suddenly, I heard, "Fly!" and I felt myself being pushed into the middle of the street. Several cars passed so close to me, I could feel the wind of their movement.

"Are you crazy?" one driver yelled out his window. Horns were honking. Everyone seemed shocked.

"If you want to kill yourself, go find another place," another driver hollered. But nobody stopped or slowed down. There was no way to get back to the sidewalk. Then the light changed, and I was able to cross the street to safety.

I could hardly believe what happened. *Who did that and why?* I turned and looked, but I did not see anyone suspicious. With my heart pounding, I hurried the final block to the courthouse, where I was met by my client, Dr. Cosma.

"Mrs. Prodan, I am so happy to see you," she said, taking my hand.

"I'm glad to see you, too," I replied. "What number is our case?" I asked, trying to return to some semblance of normalcy.

"Number two."

"Good," I said. "Then we have a few minutes to talk. Do you have your second witness ready to testify?"

"Yes. She is coming. I need to meet her at the north entrance."

"Excellent. When she arrives, bring her here," I said, anxious to have a couple of minutes to myself to calm down.

She had barely walked away when I heard a voice from behind me. "Hi, Virginia!" It was one of my colleagues, Caleope. "I saw you at the stoplight before you crossed the street to the courthouse. A tall man with a sophisticated-looking camera took a few pictures of you. Do you have a secret you'd like to tell me?" she asked conspiratorially.

"What? Are you serious? Here, across from the court-house—or at the university stoplight?" I asked.

"It was the stoplight here, across from the courthouse," she replied. But before I could ask her what the man looked like, she was flagged down by a client standing at the entrance of one of the courtrooms. "You must have a secret admirer!" She winked, dashing away.

Just then, my client returned with her witness. We spoke briefly about her case and then went to the courtroom. It was packed. As we waited for the judge and prosecutor to arrive, I noticed that four new policemen with big guns were present today in addition to the usual court guards. I paused to collect myself. I needed to focus. My client was in danger of being removed from her practice and being forced to work in the infamous Bucharest psychiatric hospital. If she refused, she would lose her medical license. If she was accused of transporting foreign goods without authorization, she would be looking at twenty-five years in jail. If the prosecutor charged her with spying for a foreign government, she could be sentenced to life in prison or execution.

I knew that both Adina's church and my own were fasting and praying on our behalf, and as the judge entered the room, I said one final prayer myself. *Please, God. Give me wisdom and courage today.* Silently I prayed Psalm 118:25. *"LORD, save us! LORD, grant us success!"*

"Please rise." Everyone rose, and the judge took his place. The first case was called. The party appeared before the judge with his attorney. He was a first-year student, studying to be an architect, and he was charged with participating in a Bible study at his friend's house. His attorney argued that his client was new to town and was confused about the purpose of the visit to his friend's home. He contended that his client was not a Christian, but a devoted and loyal young Communist.

He then produced documents of his client's activities back in his hometown as a high school Communist leader and of his extra hours of volunteer work for the Party, then asked for clemency from the prosecutor and the judge.

At the attorney's suggestion, the judge sentenced the boy to one year of Communist rehabilitation training and an extra twenty hours of volunteer work each month for the rest of his time at university. In addition, he was to report any other Christians that he encountered while at school. If he failed to do any of these things, he would be expelled and sent directly to jail. The young student stood by his attorney, scared, intimidated, and nodding.

The judge concluded with the pronouncement, "Case set for review next year."

I was disgusted to once again watch one of my colleagues acting as a puppet for the regime. I felt sick to my stomach. That poor boy didn't have an attorney. He had two prosecutors and a judge against him. A quote from Aristotle popped into my head: *"He who has overcome his fears will truly be free."*

Fear makes you a traitor, I lamented. I squeezed my fists so hard, I felt my nails dig into my palms. Angry about what I had just seen happen in front of me and scared knowing what I was going to say and do next in the same courtroom to defend my client, I prayed, *I am in the midst of lions! Lord, help me!* I reminded myself of Psalm 49:5: *"Why should I fear when evil days come, when wicked deceivers surrounded me?"*

I was so distracted, I barely noticed when the judge called my case.

"Your Honor, the accused, Dr. Adina Cosma, willfully disobeyed the Communist rules," the prosecutor began. "Not only did she refuse to worship our leader, but she also encouraged others, including her own patients, to do the same. We ask that she be punished as an example to others, that her medical license be revoked, and that she be sentenced to four years in jail. We ask that upon release, she be forced to take community reeducation classes and work as a janitor at the training facility."

As soon as the prosecutor sat down, I was up like a shot. "Your Honor, my client, Dr. Cosma, is innocent. She has the right to share a Bible with others according to Romanian Law 217." I looked straight at him. "Here is a copy of the law protecting her religious rights, including the right to share a Bible with someone," I said, handing him the copy.

"Prosecutor?" the judge said, glancing over at my colleague. "Would you care to respond?"

"Yes, Your Honor," he said, standing back up. "We can provide two more witnesses who will testify that they, too, received Bibles from Dr. Cosma. Moreover, the government can prove that those Bibles were illegally introduced into Romania and that Dr. Cosma was part of this illegal activity. Your Honor, we request time to prove those charges."

There it was. He had changed the charges, just as I had anticipated. Before I could speak, the judge agreed to the prosecutor's request and set the next court date for one month later.

I turned to find my client as white as a sheet. "Don't

panic," I told her. "I knew they would try this. Call my office tomorrow to set up a time to talk about our next step and strategy, okay?"

She nodded blankly. Seconds later, I heard the court reporter's voice. "Next case, Nina and Ovidiu Lungu."

"I represent Nina and Ovidiu Lungu, Your Honor," I said, handing him my representation documents. The door to the inmates' box opened, and Nina and Ovidiu walked in wearing orange jumpsuits. They were handcuffed and guarded by four armed policemen.

Seriously? I thought. *These are not dangerous criminals. They simply showed a movie in their own home with their family.*

The prosecutor began, "Your Honor, Nina and Ovidiu Lungu directed an underground criminal activity against the Communist government in their home. In addition, they have promoted propaganda against the socialist state that, according to Article 166 of the Romanian Criminal Code, is punishable by five to fifteen years in prison."

I could feel the heat rising in my throat.

"We have documents showing that the Lungus met regularly with others in their home with the purpose of encouraging people to rebel against our leader, and they indoctrinated others—including their own children—to become Christians as opposed to good Communists. Therefore," he concluded, "they should be severely punished and set up as an example for others."

"Your Honor," I broke in. "I want to remind the prosecutor

that according to Article 27 of the Romanian Constitution—the freedom of association—my clients are free to meet in their own homes."

"And let me remind you," the prosecutor responded, "that in Romania, citizens are guaranteed free association *except* for those associations that promote rebellion against the government. The Lungus bought the goods, the *JESUS* film, from the capitalists and promoted capitalism, which is a crime under Article 29 of the Constitution."

I fired back immediately. "I want to remind the prosecutor that religious liberty is guaranteed by the Constitution in Romania."

The prosecutor responded, "There are several limits to that. According to Decree 177 of 1948, a person can belong to a religion if that religion has been registered with the state and their activity does not stand contrary to the Constitution, to public safety and order, and to good morals. Your Honor, the Lungu family belongs to the Jehovah's Witness group, an unauthorized religious group in Romania that is well known for inspiring antisocial behavior."

As I prepared to respond, two armed guards appeared on either side of me. I continued my arguments without hesitation, but inside, I was repeatedly whispering, *Jesus*.

"Your Honor, the prosecutor is incorrect when he accuses my clients of belonging to an unauthorized group called the Jehovah's Witnesses," I argued.

Once again, the prosecutor interrupted me. "According to

Article 166 of the Criminal Code, they should be punished with up to fifteen years in jail, Your Honor."

"Your Honor," I said, my voice raised yet steady. "The prosecutor's accusations are unfounded. I solicit the court to give me time to produce documents showing that my clients belong to the official Baptist Church in Bucharest and to provide evidence that my clients and their relatives watched the *JESUS* film only in celebration of Ovidiu's birthday. This wasn't an illegal meeting in my clients' home. It was a birthday celebration. Your Honor, I believe we are still free to celebrate birthdays as we want in Romania without being accused by an overzealous prosecutor of 'illegal meetings.'"

The two armed policemen edged closer. *Are they going to arrest me?* That was when I noticed that all of the other attorneys had disappeared from the courtroom. The silence was deafening. Finally, the judge spoke.

"I will grant the defense time to produce the evidence she has referenced in her argument. We will meet again in two months to hear the new evidence. Next case."

My hands trembling, I gathered my papers and left the courtroom. It was not even noon yet, and already I had been followed, photographed, pushed into traffic, and—for all I knew—almost arrested in court. All I wanted to do was go home.

I hadn't walked half a block from the courthouse when a young man with an American accent approached me from behind.

"Excuse me, Mrs. Prodan. May I speak with you, please?

My name is Scott Edelman. I am an American attorney. I was in the courtroom today with several other friends. We admire your courage—and your work." He spoke in perfect Romanian. "We at the American embassy are aware of your fight for freedom and would like to keep in touch. Can I talk with you more tomorrow? I can come to your office—or to your home if you would prefer. I would love to meet your family, too."

Finally, I found my voice. "What about tomorrow afternoon in my home at five?"

"Perfect. See you then," he said, giving me his business card.

I looked at the card. I could not keep it; that would be too dangerous. If the *Securitate* were ever to find it in my possession, they could accuse me of being a spy and have me executed.

I would be breaking no Romanian law by meeting with Scott or having him in my office or house. No Romanian law *on record*, that is. The Communist government often threatened that there was a law, Decree 408, that forbade Romanians to have any contact with foreigners, but that law had never been published, so even attorneys had no way of knowing what it really said or if it even existed. Ceauşescu preferred it that way; secret "laws" could be interpreted and abused in any way the *Securitate* wished, and we citizens could never be sure what our rights were. So I knew it was best to keep my meetings with Scott private—even Radu did not know of them. He was out most of the time anyway, betting on his horses. With our relationship on such fragile footing, I figured the less he knew, the better.

Before I went to bed that night, I memorized Scott's phone number and then burned his card. As I settled into bed— alone, wondering when or if Radu would come home—I ran Scott's number at the embassy over and over in my mind.

That night I made the news again on Radio Free Europe and the Voice of America. This time, the reporter gave listeners more information about me, my legal background and education, and my legal arguments against the prosecutors in both cases. I was delighted that my cases were apparently of interest to an international audience, but it made me fearful of government retaliation.

Within days of my first meeting with Scott, both my cases became part of the US Department of State's reports on human rights violations in Romania. Within a month after those reports were filed, the judge dismissed the prosecutor's case against Dr. Cosma, and Nina and Ovidiu were both released.

I had an ally.

CHAPTER 12

Courage is resistance to fear,
mastery of fear—not absence of fear.

—MARK TWAIN

WITH EACH CASE, the *Securitate*'s scare tactics became more intense. I knew that following God's will would not be easy, but I never expected the kind of assignment I received next.

One Sunday afternoon when Radu was traveling to Sibiu, I took my girls to Cişmigiu Park to play with their church friends. The girls had a good time, and the outing gave me an opportunity to visit with their old Sunday school teacher, Maricia, who had just had a baby.

"May I please hold your baby, Maricia?" I asked, reaching for the little bundle in her arms.

"Of course," she responded, handing him to me. "I'll go check on the older ones."

As Maricia headed off to check on the kids, I carried her little boy over to a nice shaded bench.

"My kids like playing with your girls so much," Maricia said, returning with a jacket draped over her arm.

"Here's Andreea's jacket," she said, placing it in my lap. "It's warm enough out. She'll be fine without it." She took the pacifier from Toby's mouth, and he started crying. Leaning in as if to comfort him, she whispered, "I put a very important paper in the front pocket of Andreea's jacket. Guard it with your life. You didn't get it from me." Then, raising her voice to a more audible volume, she said, "Why are you crying?" and gave Toby back his pacifier. "There you go. Good boy," she cooed.

"Don't look at the paper now," she whispered. Then, much louder, "Look at his eyes. Aren't they beautiful?"

Frightened, I barely managed a muffled, "Yes, they are."

Taking the baby from me, Maricia turned and called out to her other children. "Costin and Martha, it's time for us to go home. Baby Toby is tired." Standing, she turned to me. "It was nice seeing you again, Virginia." As she walked away, I tightened my grip on Andreea's jacket. *What just happened? What could she possibly have given me?*

I let my girls play for a few more minutes, and then we headed back home. I couldn't wait to see the paper inside Andreea's jacket. What I found scared me to death.

*

That night I crafted a secret pocket inside my suit to carry the paper with me. Just knowing it was there made me edgy as I walked to work the next morning.

As I turned down a quiet side street, I heard someone walking behind me. Although he walked at a distance, I noticed that any time I stopped, he stopped, almost as if he *wanted* me to notice him. He was tall, athletic, and well dressed; he wore dark glasses and carried an unusual phone. From time to time he used it—it appeared—to check in with someone.

"I am at the corner of Mosilor and . . ." I heard him say.

At the stoplight, he stood beside me but did not make eye contact. I glanced over at him. He could not have been more than twenty-eight years old.

I thought about saying something to him, but before I could, I heard a voice off to my left.

"Hi, Mrs. Virginia!" It was my neighbor's maid, Nicoleta.

"Hi, Nicoleta," I replied, grateful that I was no longer alone. "I see your hands are full."

"I passed by the Alimentara store this morning, and the goods truck was there with cheese and milk," she said. "I got in line immediately, and after only two hours I bought all of this!"

"Good for you!"

"Everything is gone now. I was lucky to be there when I was." She was clearly trying to steer the conversation in a particular direction. "I can stand in line for you tomorrow if you'd like," she offered. I had paid her to stand in line for certain things in the past. "I could use the money," she added.

"That would be wonderful," I said. "The same payment as last time, yes?"

"Yes," she replied. "Thank you, Mrs. Virginia."

"If I remember correctly, you bought bananas for me last time," I said.

"Yes, I remember."

"My girls refused to eat anything but those bananas for days. If you see any, I'm sure they would love to have them again."

"Of course!" she replied, smiling.

While we were talking, I glanced around, but the gentleman who had been following me had disappeared. *Maybe he got another assignment.*

"I'll call you tomorrow," Nicoleta said.

"Thank you, Nicoleta." As we turned to go our separate ways, I heard footsteps behind me. I turned around. He was back.

My heart raced and a chill ran down my spine. I sprinted toward the first store I saw. It was a tobacco shop. The smell inside the shop was horrible, but I didn't dare leave. My stalker stood right outside the store. I tried to calm myself down. *He is just a man who happens to be walking on the same street as I am.*

Suddenly, he took off his sunglasses and stared at me. His eyes were full of rage. He reached into his pocket, snatched his phone, and dialed a number. I couldn't hear him, but he looked animated as he reported to someone on the other end.

I turned my back to him and noticed the shopkeeper watching me. The sight of the angry gentleman outside glaring at me and talking on his phone seemed to concern her. I felt trapped.

I need to call my office. Someone needs to know what's happening.

"May I use your phone, please?" I asked the shopkeeper, who was now looking frightened.

"No. You must leave now!" she replied curtly, pointing at the door.

I felt for her. And yet, I felt betrayed. Taking a deep breath, I decided to face the situation head-on. So I turned, exited the store, pushed right past the man, and continued toward my office.

He walked beside me, slowly pulling back the corner of his jacket to expose his gun. "I have killed women before." His sneer seemed to ooze evil.

I felt his sharp, burning eyes. "I am Officer Lucescu. I have killed women before." I didn't think it necessary for him to repeat that fact.

Immediately, two more *Securitate* appeared, flanking me. They were all athletic young men with stern faces. I noticed that all of them were dressed in the same style: professional black suits and dark glasses. One of them spoke continually on the phone, answering only, "Yes, sir. . . . Yes, sir."

Officer Lucescu stopped in front of me and said, "You must come with us!" At that, two more officers appeared. *Really? Five* Securitate *just for me?*

I didn't know where they were taking me. I glanced around the street, but not a soul was around. Still, I hoped someone saw these *Securitate* agents abducting me. I couldn't just disappear. They couldn't do this to me. Turning left on the next street, I saw two black, unmarked *Securitate* cars. I had seen that type of car before, from a distance, following me to my office, home, and church. *This can't be happening.* My mind immediately shot to my girls. *What will happen to them if I disappear?* Then I remembered that Radu was out of town on business. *What if something has happened to them already?*

I looked toward a few shop windows for help, with no luck. I felt alone and already forgotten. *I must help myself, but how?*

Petrified, I stepped into one of the black cars, followed by two *Securitate* officers. Nobody spoke. All the officers, including the driver, looked strong, cold, and on a mission. The other officers got into the second car, prepared to follow us. The cars sped across the city, running red lights, finally stopping at the *Securitate* headquarters—the most-feared building in all of Bucharest. From the outside, it looked like just another business, an old but inviting building. But for many people in Romania, it was the temple of death.

Officer Lucescu was in a hurry, and I had no choice but to follow him through the hall, down several stairs, and down another long hall. Everything looked clean but sinister. I shivered against the cold spirit of the place.

Each office had a tall brown door with a uniformed, armed policeman standing guard. So many of them, and all so young. They seemed proud of their jobs. I pitied them and wondered about their stories, and I imagined a day when

Romania would not need them anymore. For now, however, they were the hands and eyes of a megalomaniacal dictator.

I continued to follow Officer Lucescu through a labyrinth of hallways. Finally he opened a door to a small, dark room with no window, only a small desk and a lamp. A musty stink poured out of the room. I hesitated to follow him inside. It must have been their smallest and most isolated interrogation room. *God, help me,* I prayed. *This is the absolute worst place I have ever been.*

Several guards circled the room, looking straight at me. I'd heard horror stories from clients about those overzealous young guards-in-training who would do anything and everything to show their loyalty and determination in serving the dictator.

This could be the end of my life.

I wiped the perspiration from my face and straightened my shivering spine.

Fascinated by what appeared to him as fearlessness, Officer Lucescu grinned as he asked, "What are you going to do now?" He shone the lamplight straight into my eyes. He kept staring at me, but I couldn't see him. My face and eyes burned under the light.

I have decided to follow Jesus, no turning back. No turning back!

I put a hand over my eyes, but Officer Lucescu ordered me to look at him. Two guards moved from behind me; one restrained my hand and the other whacked my face. My body recoiled from the strike. I looked directly into the light. *Is this a joke to him? I have to be calm. I cannot let my fear take over or they will win.* I prayed the words of Psalm 56:3. *"When I am afraid, I put my trust in you."* I also prayed that the officers wouldn't search me. If they were to find the secret paper hidden in my jacket, they would shoot me for sure.

Officer Lucescu's phone rang, and he leaped from his chair to answer it. "Yes, sir. I will be there in a minute! . . . Yes, sir!" He looked worried and left in a rush.

Was that screaming voice the voice of Ceauşescu? I wondered. *It surely sounded like him. No,* I thought. *It's not possible.*

The guards stayed quiet for a while, then one of the guards sneezed. I almost blurted out, "God bless you!" but I discerned they probably wouldn't welcome God's blessing. At one point, one of the guards whispered, "She is small, but she is tough."

"How much do you want to bet that she will die within an hour?" one of the others whispered back. Then the betting commenced.

"I bet five," came a voice from behind me.

"I bet ten," said another.

I tried to drown them out with prayer.

"I am poor and needy; come quickly to me, O God. You are my help and my deliverer; LORD, do not delay" (Psalm 70:5). Another verse came to mind: *"I tell you, love your enemies and pray for those who persecute you"* (Matthew 5:44). Prompted by that verse, I began to pray for each of my captors, and as I did, an unbelievable peace invaded my soul. As time dragged on, I found myself looking forward to Officer Lucescu's

interrogation. I was determined to stay strong and tell him the truth in love about my legal work.

After all, I reasoned, *they are here by human appointment, but I am here by divine appointment. Maybe I am here so they may see Christ in me.*

Finally, Officer Lucescu returned with a handful of documents and a tape recorder. As one of the guards plugged in the tape recorder, another opened the closet door, brought out a chair, and pushed me into it. His hands were strong and cold and so close to my neck, it felt as if he wanted to choke me. Yet I sensed, for just a second, a strange kind of comfort. I held my head up and hope returned to my heart. *Fear and courage cannot live together,* I repeated to myself. *You can win this!* Still, I couldn't stop worrying about the possibility of them discovering the hidden paper inside my suit.

Again, I prayed. *O Lord, deliver me. You promised, "Call on me in the day of trouble; I will deliver you, and you will honor me"* (Psalm 50:15).

Officer Lucescu looked straight at me and said, "We are recording your admission of guilt for our leader. The judge has ordered us to transport you to the Jilava jail when we are finished."

I shuddered. Jilava was one of the worst jails in Romania.

"If you want clemency, you will cooperate," he continued. "Right now, you are looking at life in prison—if not death— for not abiding by our leader's orders."

The phone rang again, and Officer Lucescu responded, "Yes sir, Mr. President," he said, jumping up and standing at attention. His eyes were huge, and his face turned beet red. "Yes, Mr. President! Yes, sir! Of course I will do it immediately, Mr. President."

My heart stopped. The room went quiet. *Is he going to kill me immediately?* I started praying and felt peace. My mind and my soul were at rest as I held on to God's promise: *"'No weapon forged against you will prevail, and you will refute every tongue that accuses you. This is the heritage of the servants of the LORD, and this is their vindication from me,' declares the LORD"* (Isaiah 54:17).

"You are released," Officer Lucescu said. I looked behind me, thinking he was talking to one of the young officers.

Then I heard several of them saying, "What? She goes free?"

"Quiet!" he barked.

"Virginia, you are free to leave this place. I will escort you immediately to the gate," he added, suddenly smiling— almost polite.

I quickly took my briefcase and followed Officer Lucescu. We walked back through the corridors without speaking. As he opened the door to the front gate, he whispered to me, "I know what you would like to say, that you have a powerful god who saved you today from our hands. Make no mistake; our leader is bigger. Your life is still in his hands. Obey him, and you will live."

I looked straight into his eyes and softly responded, "I hope one day you will know the real God, Christ, who will make you free indeed. I pray for you, that 'you will know the truth, and the truth will set you free'" (John 8:32).

"You are crazy!" He shook his head and walked away.

"Be blessed." I said. *"Bless those who persecute you; bless and do not curse"* (Romans 12:14), I quietly reflected as he walked away.

I gently touched the right side of my suit. The paper was still there.

Lord, I praise you.

*

Safely back on the street, my mind quickly shifted to the clients I was defending that day—the Buftea Baptist Church and its pastor, Mihai Sirbu. In spite of the fact that they were under constant surveillance, Pastor Sirbu courageously welcomed visiting foreign missionaries and even encouraged them to return and bring their pastors, choirs, and youth missionaries. As a result, the Buftea Baptist Church soon became the foreign missionaries' headquarters in Romania. The government was not happy.

So the *Securitate* searched the church, intending to find some damaging evidence against the pastor and to confiscate the Bibles just received from the last group of missionaries, but nothing was found. After that the government accused Pastor Sirbu of hiding Bibles imported from the West in his home garage, but they couldn't find any proof of that. (Those Bibles had been moved by trustworthy, courageous church members before the police reached Pastor Sirbu's home.) At my request, the government had to drop the charges against

Pastor Sirbu and never had the opportunity to arrest him. But now the government wanted to punish Pastor Sirbu by demolishing the church. They sent in a "search" team of twenty *Securitate* officers to damage parts of the interior then declared the building unsafe and repeatedly refused permission for the church to make the repairs.

My incident with the *Securitate* that morning had made me late for court, and I had to hurry to avoid missing the hearing. As I raced toward the courthouse, I went over my opening argument in my mind. I had all of the required evidence and formal documentation in my briefcase—documents that I suddenly realized had been with me in the interrogation room the entire time.

I smiled, thinking about how God had protected both me and my clients that morning. Had any of the documents I was carrying been discovered, they would have been seized immediately and used against me as evidence of overt disloyalty to the dictator. *Truly,* I thought, *"he will command his angels concerning you to guard you in all your ways"* (Psalm 91:11).

As I entered the courtroom, I heard the court reporter calling my case. The room was packed.

"I am here!" I almost screamed, rushing up the center aisle. "I represent the church."

"You may begin, Counselor," the judge said.

"Your Honor, Article 30 of the Romanian Constitution grants Romanian citizens freedom of religion, and that includes not only freely worshiping in the church but also the right to maintain the building of the church. Also, under

Decree 754, the church is entitled to request approval from the city government to repair and fix the building," I began. "As the church's documents clearly reflect, the Buftea Baptist Church did request approval in a timely manner, yet the city repeatedly denied its requests without explanation. When the church leaders requested a meeting with the mayor and other city officials to seek approval, they were denied again and placed on a waiting list indefinitely. When the Voice of America publicized the case, the church was immediately given notice that the building was to be demolished. Your Honor, we are asking that you deny the city's request to demolish the church and allow the church to repair and maintain its building.

"Moreover," I continued. "If you review the paperwork, you will see that the demolition request submitted by the city is not even for the Buftea Baptist Church but the building next door to it." I brought copies of the paperwork over to the judge and the prosecutor and pointed out the clerical error.

"Unbelievable!" the prosecutor responded. "Your Honor, we made a mistake."

"Yes," the judge replied, looking over the documents. "It would appear that you did. Be more careful next time, Counselor. Your foolishness has wasted the court's time." Then he banged his gavel and proclaimed, "The demolition order against the Buftea Baptist Church is denied."

I quietly rejoiced. *The Lord confused my enemies!*

The Voice of America and Radio Free Europe both dedicated several reports to this case, each taking their own delight in the clerical snafu that undid the government's best-laid plans. To me, it was just further evidence of God's providence. The day may have started out disastrously, but thanks to God's favor, I had emerged from both trials victoriously.

That evening as I headed home, a young man with a beautiful American accent approached me on the street not far from the courthouse. I recognized him as Michael Parmly from the American embassy.

"Virginia, the ambassador and his friends would like to speak with you. Would you come with me, please?"

Before I could respond, a black car with a small American flag pulled up alongside us and stopped. Michael opened the door for me, and we both jumped in. Unlike this morning, this time I had no fear of what awaited me inside, only hopeful anticipation.

"You are safe here, Virginia," he said. "The *Securitate* cannot do anything to you now. I was in the courtroom today," he continued as the car began moving. "I admire your professionalism, wisdom, courage, and determination."

"Thank you," I responded. "I wish I could say it was all me, but the truth is, I had help," I added.

"Without question," he said, smiling.

A few moments later, we arrived at the American embassy, and the car was waved inside.

"Follow me," Michael said, stepping out of the car. I walked quickly, trying to keep up with him. Once inside, we walked down a few corridors into a spacious area where the ambassador was waiting for us. As soon as we approached him, he smiled, gave me a hug, and introduced me to the two congressmen standing beside him, Frank Wolf and Christopher Smith.

We spoke for a while about my cases, and I was surprised at how much they knew about me. I was even more surprised to learn that they not only knew about my interrogation earlier, but that they were instrumental in my release. Apparently, they had just arrived in Romania that morning, first to discuss with me the many human rights violations my cases had been highlighting and next to meet with President Ceaușescu, who was insisting there were no human rights violations in Romania. At stake was the renewal of Romania's status as a most-favored nation, and that made the *Securitate* nervous enough that they decided to let me go.

Both men were very kind, and before they excused themselves, they encouraged me with Bible verses. I was shocked. It wasn't often you encountered government leaders anywhere in Romania who knew the Bible.

My next meeting was a private one with Michael and the American ambassador. As soon as we settled into the ambassador's office, I took out the paper I had been hiding in my jacket.

"This is a very important document," I told him. "I have guarded it with my life. I had it with me today when I was interrogated by the *Securitate*. It is a miracle they didn't search me."

With shaking hands, I handed the small piece of paper to the American ambassador.

They both looked at it, astonished. "Is this what I think it is?" Michael asked.

"Yes," I confirmed. "Under Ceaușescu's orders, many Bibles have been transformed at a local paper mill into his personal toilet paper."

They turned the delicately recycled paper over in their hands. "Unbelievable!" Michael said.

"Look," the ambassador pointed out. "You can still read parts of the Bible verses here . . . and here . . . and here."

"We should get some pictures, just in case anything happens to this," Michael said.

"Absolutely," the ambassador replied. "Michael, I need you to make sure this goes directly to President Reagan's desk today."

"Yes, sir," Michael replied. And then, gently holding the paper with both hands, he left the room.

"Virginia," the ambassador said, "your courage is to be commended. Rest assured, the American embassy is watching you very closely, and we will do our best to ensure your personal safety."

That evening as Michael walked me home, several *Securitate* members followed us, but they kept their distance, and Michael assured me that they almost certainly would not arrest me again. When we got to my house, Michael asked if he could come inside and meet my family.

"I would be honored," I said.

My girls both loved Michael. He told them about his daughter, Bérengère, who was the same age as Anca, and after visiting for a few more moments, he got up to leave. "Please tell your husband I said hello. I wish I could wait a little longer, but I really must get back."

"Of course," I said, slightly embarrassed that Radu was running so late. "I understand. And thank you again for getting me home safely."

"It is my pleasure," he said.

Shortly after he left, Radu arrived.

"Daddy's home!" Andreea squealed.

"Girls, go set the table. I want to speak with Daddy for a few minutes," I said, ushering them both out of the room. "Radu, we need to talk."

"Is something wrong?" he asked. He looked exhausted. He had been away all week, traveling for a case. "I'm really tired, Virginia. The trial didn't go very well, and I have a lot of preparation to do for next week."

"You mean you're leaving again?" I asked. It seemed as though he was never home anymore. And even when he was, he wasn't. *He is taking more cases outside Bucharest. I'm sure he goes back to those horse-racing events too. Is there something new I don't see?*

"Is that a problem?" he asked, his tone somewhat accusatory.

I paused for a moment. *Should I even tell him about the interrogation? Would he even care? Might he cancel his travel plans next week if he knew?* Somehow, I doubted it. Our relationship had been strained for months. We hardly even spoke to each other anymore, and it had gotten to the point where the girls were closer to the nanny than they were to him.

"What is it, Virginia?" he said, exasperated.

I sighed.

"Nothing," I replied. "Go ahead and get ready for supper. I'll be there in a minute."

Maybe it would be better, I decided, if Radu didn't know anything about the secret document or the interrogation. That way, if the *Securitate* did execute me, at least the girls would still have one parent left.

That night while I was doing the dishes, the Voice of America was reporting on the details of my trial that day. It turned out that in addition to Michael, there were also representatives from the British, German, and Israeli embassies present as well, and all of them were reporting back to their homeland presses.

What they reported on next sent my heart into my throat. They said that America had obtained evidence that Nicolae Ceaușescu was using confiscated Bibles as his personal toilet paper.

Oh my goodness, I thought. I knew Michael and the ambassador were going to share the information I gave them with the American government, but I didn't expect to hear about it on the news so quickly.

What will happen now? If anyone from the Securitate *heard that broadcast, I could be labeled an enemy of the state. What if they figure out where the Voice of America got the information about Ceaușescu's heinous use of the confiscated Bibles? They have already threatened to kill me. What's to stop them from picking me up off the street again tomorrow? Or out of my own bed tonight?*

My pulse was racing. Every small noise from outside sent me into a panic. I checked the front door twice, then again. I tried to soothe myself by reciting some of my favorite Bible verses over and over again in my head. And yet I was awake to watch the sun rise the next morning.

*

Walking to work the next day, I passed by the American embassy. The Romanian government required us to walk on the opposite side of the street, and we were even to avoid looking at it. Still, my eyes were drawn to the giant American flag flying out front—the only symbol of freedom I had in an otherwise prisonlike existence. I was still frightened, but at least now I knew people inside the embassy and in America who cared about our fight for freedom and were looking out for me.

A few blocks later, I passed long lines of people waiting for stores to open so they could buy bread or meat. They all seemed tired, frustrated, or defeated. Some had waited in line the entire night, and yet nobody complained. That is how deep the defeatism ran in their blood. My heart wept for them, and I pondered whether fear and defeat had touched me, too.

I was lost in my thoughts when a crying child ran into me.

I bent down to talk to him, and he asked me for bread. His face was messy and red, his cheeks full of tears, and his voice loud. He looked hungry, tired, and angry, and he demanded an answer. "Where is my bread? I want bread! Can I have your bread, please?" I had none.

His mother was embarrassed. She gently said to him, "The store is all out of bread today. We have to go home." She was young, poorly dressed, and clearly desperate. She looked around for someone who would share their bread, but everyone who had gotten a loaf of bread that morning was gone already.

The boy suddenly tore himself from his mom's grip and ran to the store clerk, begging for bread. The clerk stood blocking the door with his body. He looked down at the boy and responded, "No more bread for today." The boy stood for a while, looking straight at the clerk. Neither of them said another word. Finally, he walked back to his mom, took her hand into his, and silently left. I felt helpless. *Will this boy grow up to be just another obedient, defeated citizen?*

I checked my watch and broke into a run. For the second day in a row, I was about to be late for court. I was just across from the courthouse, waiting for the light to turn green, when the sound of police sirens filled the air. The *Securitate* quickly surrounded us and loudly directed the crowd to back away from the street and toward the walls of the building. Instantly, the traffic stopped and every office closed. Workers were evacuated and pushed into the streets. No words were exchanged. Almost everyone looked down.

The silence was interrupted only by the screaming of the police as they directed and redirected us.

They picked a few people out of the crowd and took them away with no explanation provided or resistance received. *Who were those people? Were they suspected dissidents?* No one wanted to ask or know.

Then two *Securitate* demanded that we practice cheering and applauding before a car full of government officials reached our area. Small Romanian flags and signs were forced into our hands.

Cheering and touching those signs disgusted me. I felt dirty and trapped. I wanted to cry and scream, but I had heard stories of people being arrested for not smiling or being cheerful on command, and because I never knew who around me was a *Securitate* agent or an informant, I did my best to put on a happy face, hoping the whole thing would be over quickly so I could get to court. I was running late as it was, and a group of young men who had been secretly training as pastors were in danger of being jailed today.

The *Securitate* had approached these men individually and requested that they spy on their congregations. The men refused to collaborate, so the *Securitate* decided to change their tactics. The prosecutor had charged the men with transporting and sharing Bibles when they visited people's homes as part of their pastoral training.

My feet were killing me. *High heels were not a smart choice.* I wanted to take them off, but I didn't want to be disrespectful to the *Securitate*, so I shifted from one foot to the other for almost two hours, and *still* there was no sign of the Communist officials. Finally, after two and a half hours, we were told to return the flags and signs and be on our way. Later, I heard that the officials had decided to take another street.

As soon as I got inside the courthouse, Natalia, the secretary for the president of the Bucharest Bar Association, approached me. "President Gica Teodosi wants to see you immediately. Please follow me."

I tried making small talk. "Is everything okay with him? I know he had a heart attack last year."

"Yes, everything is okay—*with him.*"

I worried about Gica's family, but judging by Natalia's distant tone, I didn't say more. I kept thinking about his wife's health, as she had attempted suicide twice in the last year.

I had met Gica Teodosi through the Bucharest Bar Association a few years back, and we quickly became close friends. He and his wife were at our wedding, and he was even Anca's godfather. The relationship became a little more distant after I became a Christian, but we still enjoyed seeing each other from time to time.

Natalia asked me to wait in the reception area until she announced my presence. A few seconds later, she returned. "The president is ready to see you."

"Good morning, Gica! How are you?" I said, entering the office.

He stood and smiled. "It's nice to see you, Virginia. Please, have a seat. I just finished a conversation with one of your old law school professors, Radu Popescu. He asked me about you. He is a big fan of yours," he continued. "Tell me, how is my goddaughter? I still remember when we secretly baptized her in your home."

Then before I could respond, he abruptly raised his voice and admonished me for taking cases that no loyal Communist lawyer would take.

"I told you to stop defending those churches and radical Christians!" he bellowed. "You shall be a loyal Romanian attorney!" His face turned bright red, and for a minute, I thought he was having another heart attack. I thought about running for help, when the door behind me burst opened and four young *Securitate* rushed in and ordered me to follow them.

I glanced back at Gica. Winded from shouting, he lowered his head and waved me away. The *Securitate* ushered me into a car and drove me to an office across town. Once there, they grilled me about my involvement with Voice of America and the American embassy.

"One minute they are talking about how brilliantly you performed in court and the next they are announcing that they have evidence that Ceaușescu turns Bibles into his personal toilet paper," one of them said sternly. "And now there is talk that Romania may lose its most-favored-nation status from America."

"We have seen you talking with members of the American embassy," another broke in. "And we know that one of them was recently in your home. You realize that is in direct violation of Decree 408, forbidding Romanian citizens to have any association with foreigners."

They were putting the pieces together. I was starting to panic. Radio Free Europe and the Voice of America reported almost daily about people being expelled from the Communist Party, being arrested, or disappearing altogether after granting interviews with Western newspapers or speaking with foreigners.

"We know about your association with the Western representatives, who only come into the courtroom for *your* cases," he continued. "You are frequently referenced on Voice of America and Free Europe. You even had a meeting with the American ambassador and Congressmen Wolf and Smith at the American embassy."

My God, I thought. *They know everything.*

As if reading my mind, the largest of the officers said, "Are you surprised we know this? We have people everywhere. According to Decree 408, we can arrest you immediately."

He pushed a sheet of paper across the table at me. I skimmed it. It was a press release stating that the American congressmen had lied about there being any violations of human rights in Romania and that they had used me to spread their capitalist propaganda against my will.

"You will sign this release," he said, holding out a pen. When I paused to read the release more closely, he became angry.

"America can take away our most-favored-nation status! Don't you understand? That is because of you! Now sign here!"

Do they know about the paper proving Ceaușescu trans-formed Bibles into his personal toilet paper? Is that the reason America might take away the most-favored-nation status?

Heaven knows America had plenty of other reasons to do it. Unfortunately, my association with the two congressmen, coming immediately before the threat of status change, put me under suspicion.

"Sign it!" the officer again demanded.

As terrified as I was of the consequences of not signing the release, I was even more frightened of God's consequences if I did. *"Do not be terrified by them, or I will terrify you before them,"* I thought, recalling Jeremiah 1:17.

"No, I will not sign it," I stated firmly.

If God is with me, who can be against me?

The officers were not happy with my response. But some-how they were restrained in their physical actions toward me. They only screamed and pounded on the table.

Everything stopped when the phone rang.

"Yes, Mr. President. Surely, Mr. President!" The officer on the phone jumped up, saluting.

I recognized the screaming voice on the other end of the line instantly. It was Ceaușescu.

I felt my death approaching rapidly.

Lord, I prayed, *"my times are in your hands; deliver me from the hands of my enemies, from those who pursue me"* (Psalm 31:15).

"Yes, Mr. President; I will personally report!" the officer responded, his face turning red.

The room went deathly quiet.

The red-faced officer straightened his jacket, sat down at the table, and very calmly offered me a bribe.

Ah . . . I thought. *They are changing tactics.*

They promised me a bigger house in an exclusive Communist leaders' area and a brand-new car. When I refused, they threatened to kill me and my family.

"Sign here!" two officers flanked me on either side and screamed at me, just inches from my face. "We can take you directly to Jilava jail!"

"No," I responded.

Suddenly, the officer to my left kicked the chair out from beneath me, sending me to the floor and the chair into the wall, where it shattered into a dozen pieces. I smacked my head hard on the floor, and I could taste blood filling my mouth. I put my hand up over my mouth as the room began to spin.

Another officer helped me get up.

"I swear I will kill you today," he said. "Now sign here!"

I remained silent and tried to regain my composure.

"I will take it from here," said a fifth officer, who had just entered the room.

"Here," he said, offering me a chair. "Have a seat." Then he nodded at the others, letting them know it was time for them to leave. Once we were alone, save for the most senior-looking officer who stood guard by the door, he leaned in and said, "Listen, my colleagues are hot-tempered guys. What would it take for you to sign this release? You know we can provide you with a new car. Is there a particular color you would like?"

Everything has a price for them, I thought.

"How about a nice vacation. As far as I know—and I know a lot—you have not had a decent vacation for a long time. We could even arrange for you to travel outside Romania—*if* you stop defending churches and all those crazy religious people."

He waited for my answer.

"No," I responded.

His face hardened. "No? Okay, Mrs. Prodan. You just signed your own death papers."

"My colleague is serious," said the officer guarding the door. "He is going to kill you and your girls."

Terror pierced my soul. *Lord, my life is in your hands. Please protect my girls.*

"You can go now," he said, pointing to the door. The other officer stepped aside. "But remember, we will be watching every move you make," he said menacingly. "Your life is in our hands."

As I made my way back onto the street, my entire body was trembling. They could very easily have killed me. But as dangerous as it was to keep me alive, it would have been more dangerous to kill me—and they knew that. In addition to the *Securitate*, the American ambassador, two congressmen, and multiple international radio networks were also watching my every move, and if something were to happen to me, the repercussions would be devastating. Ceaușescu knew the most-favored-nation status was America's way of protecting against human-rights violations and keeping him in check, but he desperately needed that status from America. Without it, Romania would lose hundreds of millions of dollars in trade revenue. Romania was already a struggling nation. Losing trade relations with America would be the Communist Party's death knell.

It was painfully simple.

As I lived and died, so, too, did Romania.

CHAPTER 13

"Who will let you?"

"That's not the point. The point is, who will stop me?"

—AYN RAND, *The Fountainhead*

To SAY THAT IT HAD BEEN an exhausting week would be a gross understatement. Between the two interrogations, the meetings with the American embassy, and a full complement of court cases, I was looking forward to spending a quiet evening at home with the girls.

As I was packing up my things to leave the office, my secretary called to tell me that Andreea's teacher had called and wanted to see me at the school this afternoon.

"Is Andreea okay?" I asked, my nerves still on edge.

"She didn't say," she replied. "But I'm sure if it were an emergency, she would have said something."

Lord, give me strength, I prayed as I headed out the door.

When I got to the school, the teacher invited me into her classroom, where I awkwardly squeezed into one of the child-sized desks.

"Thank you for coming, Mrs. Prodan," she said. "I wanted to speak with you about a problem I had with Andreea today. We were studying Darwin and evolution, and I asked the class to write a few sentences about what they had learned and then share them with the class."

"Was she disruptive?" I asked.

"Yes and no," the teacher responded. "When I asked Andreea to share what she had written, she shared this." She began reading from a sheet of paper. "'We are beautifully and wonderfully made. We are unique. There will never be, in the entire universe, one person that is identical to another. We are not animals. We are created by our God and in his image. God created us to reflect him and his love. He put people in charge of all animals. God loves each one of us. That lesson that said we are animals was wrong.'"

I have to admit, my heart swelled with joy upon hearing Andreea's words. Not only was she solid in her faith, but to openly challenge the falsehood of the day's lesson showed great courage and conviction on her part. As a parent and a Christian, I could not have been more proud. Her teacher, on the other hand, was not in the least bit pleased or impressed.

"Naturally, Andreea's essay raised all kinds of questions from the class," she continued.

"'What does she mean we are unique?'" she said, imitating one of the students. "'And what does she mean we are all

beautifully and wonderfully made? I have seen ugly people,'"
she said, parroting another. "'Who is God? Is she talking
about our leader?'"

She looked exasperated.

"I had no choice but to stop the presentations and force
the class to copy the entire lesson on evolution, word for
word, in their notebooks."

I could sense the tension and frustration in her voice
and eyes. We stared at each other in silence for a moment.
I wasn't sure what to say. I wanted to tell her I was proud of
what Andreea had written, but I knew that was not what she
wanted to hear.

"Look," she said, lowering her voice to a whisper. "When
I was Andreea's age, I also learned about God and Creation.
But we are living in a different time now. Andreea needs to
keep the truth to herself and follow my class lessons and
instructions. She cannot confuse the other students. *We* are
in charge of the truth now."

I wanted to say, "You are teaching my child to lie. What
kind of teacher are you?" But I knew better. She would have
reported me, and then the government might have taken
the girls away from me. So I quickly and quietly prayed for
wisdom and love.

"If you had been in Andreea's place, what would you have
said?" I asked calmly.

Her answer surprised me.

Whispering, she said, "I don't know. My parents raised
me the same way you have raised Andreea. I used to believe

the same things as you. I *still* believe, but if I admit that, I will lose my job, and I am only two months away from retiring."

I felt for her.

"Would you explain that to Andreea?" she asked. "Ask her to please keep her beliefs to herself while she is in my class?"

I sat silently. I had worked so hard to teach my girls about God, the Bible, and the importance of standing up for your beliefs. How could I now tell them to keep quiet? *How hypocritical would that be?*

I looked at Andreea's teacher. I could see the fear in her eyes. It was a fear I knew all too well. After all, if there was anyone who understood the danger inherent in making one's faith known, it was me. I had almost been killed twice this week for standing up for my faith. Was it fair for me to expect others to do the same?

Before I could respond, she spoke again. "After I retire, I would love to have one of those Bible picture books Andreea told me about—for my grandkids."

"Of course," I said reassuringly. "And yes, I will speak to Andreea. I will tell her that you are also a believer, but that you would like to keep your shared belief a secret until the end of the school year."

I could see the relief wash over her face.

"Thank you, Mrs. Prodan."

I really did feel for her. In many ways, we were the same—two jailed souls, trapped within a Communist prison. The only difference was that she chose to submit to her captor, while I had chosen to fight. I promised myself I would pray for her.

Walking home, I thought about how I would break the news to Andreea. She wanted so much to share the gospel with others. I had to find a way to explain to my girls that there were some Christians who considered their jobs more important than Christ and that Andreea's teacher was one of them. *How do I do that without scaring the girls or putting down a teacher?*

Over the weekend, I spoke separately with both girls about it. Then we talked about it together. I was surprised by their reaction, a rather blasé, "Okay." I hoped they understood.

I also had a talk with them about being careful when they answer people's questions about what we say at home, who visits us, and so on. I thought I had done a good job, until the Sunday when my neighbor whose daughter frequently played with my girls stopped me on the street.

"Virginia, your girls are so cute! I was admiring their haircuts, and when I asked them who their hairstylist was, they both responded at once, 'We don't know.' When I told them that I would ask you, they both responded, 'Mom forgot it too.'"

I forced a smile, but my heart was filled with pain. *Am I just confusing my girls? How can I help them understand the circumstances we live in?*

God, help me to know what the right thing to do is.

*

Almost a year and a half after Scott Edelman visited my home, his two-year term at the American embassy ended, and he was recalled to America. Before leaving, though, he introduced me to another member of the embassy team, Susan Sutton, a young Texan from El Paso who spoke fluent Romanian and was extremely knowledgeable about my country and its current regime. Susan was tall and slim with short hair and a perpetual smile. She was in the courtroom for almost all of my cases. She seldom took notes, but she always remembered every detail.

One day Susan invited me to a special reception at the American embassy to meet the new ambassador, Roger Kirk, and his staff.

Ever cognizant of the dangers for me, she promised, "I can come and pick you up, to make sure you get to the American embassy's reception safely."

For a moment I was unsure. "I cannot predict what the *Securitate* will do if they see you. I think I'd better come alone."

"In that case, someone from the embassy will watch discreetly to make sure you are not stopped or arrested," she said.

Then she added a detail that made me shiver. "Some of the workers hired for this special reception—waitresses, drivers, cleaning helpers—are Romanians."

I voiced the concern we both knew was true. "Remember, they have to report everything to the *Securitate*."

She was not fazed. "If you perceive me or anyone else from the embassy changing the conversation, just follow our lead."

The evening of the reception, two *Securitate* followed me as I walked to the American embassy. They backed off slightly, however, when they saw the uniformed Marine posted at the gate. Once I was safely inside, Susan, smiling as always, approached me.

"Hi, Virginia. You made it!" she said, giving me a small hug. "This time you were followed not only by the *Securitate* but also by two of our staff members. We wanted to make sure you would get here safely." She winked at me.

Being inside the embassy was like entering a different world. The rooms were large and tastefully decorated. The style was simple and elegant, with American flags proudly displayed throughout. Each room was decorated with pictures from different parts of America—Washington, DC; Texas; Chicago; Hawaii. It struck me that the entire country was on display, freedom was on display, even prosperity was on display, but there was not one individual person on display. Not one picture of an American president, past or present. It was such a stark contrast to all of the other government buildings I had been in, which were filled with photos of Ceaușescu, Lenin, Castro, and other Communist leaders.

Just as Susan had said, food and drinks were served by Romanians, all of whom spoke excellent English. They were all well dressed, attentive, and looked very friendly, but I recognized their mission. Carrying plates from one part of the room to another, they purposefully paused a little longer in certain spots.

"What kind of drink would you like?" one waiter asked me in perfect English.

"Water," I responded with my heavy Romanian accent.

"Okay." He stared at me. I knew that look. It said, *Be a*

good Romanian patriot! I had seen that look and heard those words many times from the *Securitate*. I knew I had to watch for *Securitate* among the crowd. Likely it would be someone who was trying to blend in.

The Americans were easy to spot. They were healthy looking, smiling, and friendly. *Is that what freedom and liberty look like?* I wondered. Among the Romanian people you would encounter on the streets, in the courthouse, or in stores, only the Christians were hopeful and smiling. But none of them had the same American smile or friendliness.

Later that evening, Susan introduced me to the new ambassador, who spoke beautiful Romanian.

I shook his hand. "Nice to meet you, Mr. Ambassador."

"You look surprised that I speak Romanian." He smiled and winked. "I have to. I don't want to be sold down the river," he joked. "I walk around town a lot after work and try to blend in. Speaking Romanian helps a lot. I've also learned to read between the lines and discern people's body language, as speaking the truth freely is rare here—especially on the streets."

Unaware of where each of the waiters were at the moment, I worded my response carefully. "You are a smart diplomat to do all that, helping not only America, but us, too."

Sensing my hesitancy, he invited Susan and me to his office to continue our conversation.

"I assure you that all the detailed updates you have provided regarding your religious and human-rights cases, both old and new, will help America and Romania's relationship," he stated. "I know for sure it will help us prepare for my meeting with President Ceaușescu this week."

"I certainly hope so, Mr. Ambassador," I responded.

"We will continue to send Susan and other American embassy staff to each one of your court cases," he continued. "We know the *Securitate* might try to arrest you—even silence you more drastically."

The concern about a permanent "silencing" was not unwarranted. The fact that the Voice of America and Radio Free Europe covered my cases gave me some protection—as long as Ceaușescu needed the most-favored-nation status from America, he couldn't afford to be suspected of harming me. But that protection was by no means absolute. Over the years, Ceaușescu had been behind several failed assassination attempts to silence "outside dissidents" like Paul Goma, Monica Lovinescu, and Emil Georgescu—exiled from Romania but continuing to criticize Ceaușescu via the Voice of America and Radio Free Europe. It would be even easier to attack someone within Romania itself.

"Michael Butler will escort you back home this evening," the ambassador assured me. "You should ask him about his encounter with the *Securitate*. Rest assured that I will make sure it *never* happens again." The ambassador's face took on a look of determination as he said that.

Michael Butler was a tall, strong, and intelligent young man. I will never forget what he told me that night.

"I was taking pictures of government workers who were in the process of demolishing a two-hundred-year-old

Orthodox church in Bucharest to make room for Ceauşescu's palace, and four *Securitate* came up and arrested me," he began. "I said, 'I am an American citizen. I have my credentials here.' Then I showed them my documents. One officer pulled my camera away from me, took out the roll of film, and smashed the camera in front of me. I said, 'You cannot do this to an American diplomat,' and they just said, 'Watch us! We can do whatever we want to whomever we want—including American diplomats.'"

I stifled a gasp.

"The next thing I knew," Michael continued, "I was on the ground with my hands handcuffed behind me. Then I was taken to a *Securitate* interrogation room."

"Then we have something in common," I said. "I was arrested and interrogated by the *Securitate* too!"

He shook his head in disbelief.

"After a few hours, I was released. The next day, they lied to the ambassador, claiming they were not aware that I was an American diplomat. And they apologized for the destruction of my camera." I could hear the anger in his voice. "Liars!" he growled.

"Congratulations, Michael," I said, reaching over to shake his hand. "Soon you might be considered persona non grata like me." We both laughed at the absurdity of the situation.

*

The next day, it was back to business as usual. I spent the morning in consultation with a few members of an Evangelical

Lutheran church in Sibiu. Like the Baptist church I had just defended, they had been requesting permission from the government for years to repair and expand their church building, but the government refused. Desperate to make the necessary repairs and addition, individual members of the church built a new section in secret. Once again, everything was done with the financial support and manpower of its members. Now the government wanted to demolish the building and throw the pastors and everyone who participated into jail.

The case was scheduled to go to trial in Sibiu, almost four hours northwest of Bucharest, the next day.

"That only gives me a few hours to prepare," I told them. "I'm not sure if I can look over all those documents and be fully prepared by tomorrow."

They appeared desperate.

"We ask you to take our case and defend us, even if it is only to show your support," the pastor implored. "Please. For years we have tried and failed to find an attorney who would agree to defend us."

Under those terms, I agreed to represent them. That night, the pastor and two other members of the church stayed in Bucharest to make sure I had someone to drive me to Sibiu the next morning, just in case the *Securitate* decided to slash my tires.

With Radu once again out of town, I arranged for Maria, our nanny, to come early the next morning to take care of the girls. After I had gotten both of them to bed for the evening, I spent the next several hours reviewing the material the pastor had given me. Mostly, however, I prayed. *Lord, help me to get through whatever material is necessary for tomorrow.*

Surprisingly, the trip out to Sibiu was uneventful. As I entered the courtroom, I was greeted by the prosecutor, who had been on the case from the beginning. Though his greeting was polite, his expression clearly communicated, *You are dead. Done. Finished!*

I responded with a polite smile and a silent prayer.

In his opening remarks, the prosecutor asked the court to demolish not just the new addition, but the entire church, just to teach the pastor and his congregation a lesson. He also asked for an enormous fine—to be paid that day. Further, he asked that if the pastor was unable to pay the fine immediately, that the police arrest him as well as all the members participating in this "conspiracy against the government" on the spot. He presented no documents and no evidence. His only foundation was his spoken accusation.

I presented the documentation verifying the pastor's repeated requests to the government for permission to repair and expand their building, as well as proof that they had dutifully followed the law in appealing each rejection. I also presented evidence that over time, the church's building had deteriorated to the point that it had become a danger to its members, and I documented the need for the expansion.

Frankly, given how little time I'd had to prepare, I was stunned at my ability to pull all of this documentation out right when I needed it—or that I even remembered it at all. I had no doubt that God was orchestrating everything.

After I finished, the court broke to verify all of the evidence, exhibits, and documentation I had presented. Two hours later, they decided in favor of the church. I was elated. Not only was it a victory for my clients and the church, but my personal faith was reinvigorated by the knowledge that God had been working through me the entire morning, guiding my words, organizing my thoughts, and helping me find just the right files when I needed them.

I all but floated back to Bucharest that evening. Meditating on the assurance of Philippians 4:13—"I can do all things through Christ who strengthens me" (NKJV)—I felt as though I could take on the *Securitate* as well as Ceaușescu all by myself—with God!

*

As word of my success continued to be spread by the Voice of America, Radio Free Europe, and throughout the Christian underground, more and more churches started coming to me for help—many, like the church in Sibiu, from cities outside of Bucharest.

For example, shortly after I finished defending the Sibiu church, a Pentecostal church in Bistrița called asking for help. This one was close to being demolished because the government had declared it unsafe and refused the church's repeated requests to repair it.

So that's Ceaușescu's plan, I thought. *Slowly demolish all the churches until none are left.*

I visited the church to examine the situation myself. Like the others, when the government refused their repeated requests, the individual members took it upon themselves to start making the necessary repairs.

Ceaușescu doesn't realize who he's up against.

Immediately I prepared the necessary paperwork and filed a suit against the Bistrița city government.

When I arrived in Bistrița the following month, I found that the government had posted police cars and bulldozers at each corner of the church. They were planning to demolish the church *before* the trial the next day.

The government was furious and embarrassed because the Pentecostal church members had secretly finished the entire renovation long before the church spies informed the government about it. Now, I was in the position of proving that the church's building was safe.

Quickly, the pastor, the majority of the church members, and I assembled at the building, vowing to occupy the church and worship there until the government either abandoned their plans or dared to demolish the building with us inside.

When word of our occupation got back to the American embassy, the Voice of America and Radio Free Europe reported on the story; members of the American, British, Jewish, and French embassies descended upon Bistrița with foreign reporters and photographers; and soon media outlets from all over the world were broadcasting our peaceful protest.

Soon the Romanian government had no choice but to

stop the demolition and allow me to defend the church in court the next day. Needless to say, the courtroom was full of foreign reporters and diplomats.

After I made my argument, the judge—in an effort to reduce the tension—announced that he would be making a decision that day. True to his word, within an hour, he ruled in favor of the church.

Spiritually and professionally, I was soaring. However, all of the attention my cases had been receiving from the foreign press put my physical life in grave danger. Many days I awoke to find that my tires had been slashed overnight. And I had to be accompanied by at least two bodyguards at all times. I was constantly amazed at how readily young church members would risk their lives to protect me and sacrifice their own meager savings to help replace my tires time and time again. Just as I put myself at risk to protect and defend them, they did the same for me. It was as though we had formed our own little *Securitate* to combat that of the government. We even learned how to outsmart the *Securitate* and beat them at their own game.

For instance, when yet another Baptist church came under pressure from the government to be demolished, its pastor, Peter Dugulescu, reached out to me.

Dugulescu and his congregation were aware that the *Securitate* had slashed my tires several times to prevent me from traveling to distant cases, so we arranged to stop randomly in different cities and change cars to throw them off the scent. The plan worked beautifully until the final leg of our journey, when we caught a glimpse of a black *Securitate* car following close behind us. When we turned the corner, however, we noticed that the *Securitate* were being followed by an American embassy car. *God bless our allies at the American embassy,* I prayed.

The morning of the trial, we met at the church for a short prayer and then headed over to the courthouse. No sooner had we arrived than a car stopped in front of us. Four *Securitate* got out and rushed straight toward us. One of them started shouting, "We don't know how you managed to get your attorney here, but we have heard that there is someone else coming—someone named Maranatha. Whoever he is, he is not welcome here!"

I could hardly stop myself from laughing. Apparently the *Securitate* had planted a spy at our prayer meeting, and he overheard us saying that we were not afraid because "Maranatha! He is coming!" What the spy didn't know was that Maranatha means "our Lord is coming." So while we were readying ourselves for our day in court, the *Securitate* were frantically scrambling to prepare for—of all things—*the coming of our Lord.*

Once again, we won the case. Not only was the church able to remain, but they were allowed to add to their building over time. Once again, the *Securitate* followed us all the way back to Bucharest. And yet again, they were followed themselves by people from the American embassy. It was a most peculiar little parade of travelers. We even stopped and had dinner at the same restaurant.

After hours of traveling, it was good to be home. I spent a few minutes catching up with Maria and the girls, then changed my clothes and collapsed into bed. Hours later, I was awakened by someone pounding on the door of our home.

Still half asleep, I staggered to the front door.

"Who is it?" I asked.

"Police. Open up! We have a search warrant for your house."

Instantly awake, I ran to the phone to call the embassy, but the phone was dead.

When the pounding continued, I opened the door, and six strong men armed with guns abruptly thrust documents in my face and pushed their way inside. I closed the door after them and looked at my watch. It was four thirty in the morning.

"We heard you have gold, guns, and American currency in your home!" the officer in charge barked. Under Communist law, it was illegal to possess gold, guns, or foreign currency—in particular, American dollars. Only the government and its elite had that privilege.

I watched as they moved from room to room, snatching books off bookshelves, opening every cabinet, and throwing everything they could find to the floor. It took them only moments to make a shambles of my bedroom. They even made sure all my lingerie was exposed, and then they made jokes about it.

The noise woke my girls as well. They were crying and frightened.

I wanted to go calm them down, but I didn't want to leave the *Securitate* alone. I had heard stories from my clients about how the *Securitate* had planted incriminating evidence during their "search" and then arrested the homeowners for it. Angry, embarrassed, and emboldened, I confronted them.

"You asked if I have any illegal gold, money, or guns in my house, and the answer is no!" I shouted. "If you came with the intention of placing those items here and later accusing me of having them, I will report it to the embassy."

A *Securitate* officer who was playing with Anca's flute immediately froze, his eyes wide with shock. Soon they all stopped and looked at me. For a second, they were intimidated by my courage. But it didn't take them long to regroup.

I reminded myself, *"The Lord is my Shepherd"—and the girls need my attention.*

"Girls," I said calmly, walking over to them, "the police are here to search the house." Then as reassuringly as possible, I whispered, "God will protect us. Pray Psalm 23 to each other and pray for me, too, okay? I want you to stay in your room. Once they finish out here, they will probably come and search your room, too, but I will be here. I promise." I hugged and kissed them, and then got them started on Psalm 23 before I backed out of the room and closed the door.

"The Lord is my Shepherd. . . ."

Returning to the room where the officers were still searching, I quickly said a prayer to encourage myself. *"Guard my life, for I am faithful to you"* (Psalm 86:2). At the end of their search, the officers admitted they didn't find anything and left, but before they did, one of them said, "We searched your office a few hours ago. You might need to clean that, too."

I closed the door after them. It was seven thirty a.m. The house was in shambles.

Still, I could not believe that I was not arrested, and I praised God for that. I had been spared again. *But for how long?*

I went up to the girls' room to check on them, and we hugged and praised God together. Psalm 84:12 came to my mind: *"Lord Almighty, blessed is the one who trusts in you."*

"Why do they hate us, Mom?" Anca asked.

"Some people just don't like Jesus," I explained. "And they don't like people who do." It was a simple explanation, but for now, it would have to suffice. "Come on," I said. "You can sleep with me for a while." We all climbed into my bed together and sang:

> *Nu te-ndoi, ci crede că după orice nor*
> *E-un soare și mai dulce, și mai strălucitor*

> Don't doubt but believe that behind every dark moment in your life
> There is the Son of God victorious and ready to help you.

Soon both girls fell asleep, while I lay awake thinking of ways to respond to the questions they would inevitably have about what had happened tonight.

A few hours later, I awoke and realized I was already late for an appointment. I took a quick shower and was dressed and ready to leave just as Maria arrived. I told her what had happened and assured her that everything would be okay.

"When the girls wake up, ask them to help you clean their room," I said. "I will do the rest after work."

When I opened the front door, I saw several *Securitate* officers smoking and pacing in front of the house. As soon as I walked outside, they followed me, then two of them approached me.

"Come with us," they said, shoving me into a waiting black car.

When we arrived at the *Securitate* headquarters, I noticed several of my clients waiting in line in front of an office, filling out paperwork as directed by four officers.

I waved to them, and an officer slapped my hand and ordered me to follow him into the next office. He left me with a young officer who gave me paperwork to fill out. As I was responding to their questions, the door opened, and another officer came inside.

"I am Officer Pascu," the officer barked, "and you will do as I say. Otherwise, I have methods to make you talk." He leaned in closely. "And they always work." He nodded at the younger officer, who quietly left the office, closing the door behind him.

Officer Pascu placed a document in front of me, and as soon as I tried to read it, he slammed his fist down in the middle of it. "I prepared this paper for you. You only have to sign it!" he shouted. When I tried again to read the document, he shook my chair violently. "If you don't sign this paper saying that you will stop defending Christians and churches, I will kill you!"

"Love your enemies and pray for those who persecute you" (Matthew 5:44), I reminded myself.

"No," I said calmly but firmly.

He slammed his palm into the back of my head so hard that my face hit the desk.

"No," I repeated. Then he continued pounding my face into the desk until my blood covered the paper lying there. I felt light-headed and confused. Silently I prayed, *"Keep me safe, my God, for in you I take refuge"* (Psalm 16:1).

The door opened again, and another *Securitate* officer came inside with paper napkins and a wet cloth.

"He didn't mean to do that," he said, taking all the bloody paper from the desk and throwing it in the trash can. "He is just trying to help you be a good Communist attorney." Then he showed Officer Pascu the door.

I hated when they played good cop, bad cop. I never knew which one was more dangerous. So I quietly prayed for them and for myself. I needed peace. But more than that, I needed to have love for them.

Lord, have mercy on their souls.

"I am Officer Amanar." I never knew if those names were real. He stood across the table from me, as if he were visiting with an old friend.

"My wife and I have two girls the same age as yours—Maria

and Cristina. We just returned from vacation in Rome. My girls enjoyed it so much. I bet your girls would like it too."

Ah . . . I thought. *He's going to try to bribe me with fancy vacations.*

He also told me stories about how his girls enjoyed many privileges because of his loyalty to the government. Then he began to talk about my daughters. I trembled at how much he knew about them.

"Did you know that Anca wandered away from her classmates on a school trip once? We could have kidnapped her, but we decided not to. And so you know," he continued, "the homeless guy who attempted to kill you by pushing you into the traffic was also one of us. You survived that day, but think about your family," he added with a sinister air. "We have noticed that your husband is away a lot. And that woman who watches your girls? She would be no match for our officers."

I tried to ignore him and pray. *"In God I trust and am not afraid. What can man do to me?"* (Psalm 56:11). When Officer Amanar decided he had tortured me enough, he let me go, but not before he reminded me to think again about my girls.

"I noticed at least two times that your girls walked back home from school alone. That could be very dangerous." Then he came right up beside me and whispered in my ear, "They love to play hide-and-seek with their neighbors, yes? They hide. We seek!" He snickered.

I felt a shiver run through my entire body. *"My flesh and*

my heart may fail, but God is the strength of my heart and my portion forever" (Psalm 73:26), I reminded myself. I quickly prayed for Officer Amanar.

He then walked with me down the hall past the line of my clients. I recognized all of them, even though I hadn't seen many of them since I'd defended them years earlier. I looked at each one, and they looked back at me, some in horror and some with hope. *Why are they all here?* As soon as I was clear of the building and breathing fresh air again, I rushed to my office to treat my wounds.

Later that afternoon, I received a call from Adina Cosma, one of my clients whom I had seen at the *Securitate* headquarters.

"I was just released after four hours of interrogation," she said. "I saw many of your clients there, and all of us had been interrogated by the government, threatened, or bribed in an attempt to get us to sign a complaint against you. I want you to know that I didn't sign the complaint."

"Thank you, Adina," I said. "I am grateful for your courage and your faithfulness."

"You are welcome, Mrs. Virginia. It is the very least I could do," she said before she hung up.

I felt my blood rush to my head. *So that's what they were doing there. What if the* Securitate *succeed in finding just one former client who is willing to work with them? They know everything about my schedule, my girls, their friends. And they know Radu is rarely if ever at home. What could happen?*

With my heart aching, I began to pray, *My salvation and*

my honor depend on you, God; you are my mighty rock, my refuge (from Psalm 62:7). Anxious to see and hold my girls, I closed my files and got ready to leave for home.

Just then, Miruna, my legal assistant, peeked into my office doorway.

"A big man in the waiting room says he wants to discuss a case." She shrugged. "That's all he will tell me."

Will this day never end? I thought. "Go home, Miruna. I'll see how I can help him."

I followed her to the reception room and invited the tall, muscular man waiting there to follow me. As he entered my office, he ran his huge hand over the silver doorplate reading, *Virginia Prodan, Attorney.* Then he closed the door behind him. I was taken aback at how enormous he was. As he sat down in front of my desk, his eyes seemed to bore a hole straight through me, and a sneer began to turn at the corner of his mouth.

Securitate! My blood ran cold. *How could I have been so careless?*

Slowly, he pulled back his coat and reached into a shoulder holster, withdrawing a gun.

"You have failed to heed the warnings you've been given," he said, pointing the gun toward me. "I've come here to finish the matter once and for all."

He flexed his fingers, and I heard the distinctive click of a trigger cocking into place.

"I am here to kill you."

My hands shook. Fight-or-flight instincts pinged in my

brain. I couldn't fight. At barely five feet tall, I was no match for this monster. Nor could I flee; I'd never get past him to the closed door. My chin trembled. An image flashed through my mind: my assistant arriving in the morning and finding my lifeless body on the floor of my office.

As my mind raced, the gunman explained in a calm, almost businesslike tone, exactly how he would carry out my execution.

My mind continued to race. *I could scream, but who would hear me?* This late in the day, the building would be almost empty. My assassin had planned it that way, of course, so that no one could come to my aid. Fear froze me to my chair. Nothing—not interrogations or arrest—had rendered me so desperate and helpless. This assassin's stone-faced determination and gleaming gun decreed that I'd finally met my end.

Warnings from friends and family rang in my ears. They had foretold this would happen if I continued to defy the Ceauşescu government. I knew that someday I'd pay the ultimate consequence for my actions—but I never considered it would be *this* day.

Not able to face the dark, angry eyes of the man, I stared at intricate designs in the rug beneath my feet. I was alone with my killer. And yet, I was not. *Jesus!* I began silent, fervent prayers, recalling God's promises. His Spirit breathed peace into my panicked heart. Then I sensed his message in my spirit: *Share the gospel.*

Setting aside what might happen to me or my family, I considered the man before me. Behind those hate-filled eyes was a creation of God. He had an immortal soul, and he needed to know about the love God has shown in Jesus Christ. At once emboldened, I met my killer's eyes. "Have you ever asked yourself 'Why do I exist?' or 'Why am I here?' or 'What is the meaning of my life?' I once asked myself those questions." My voice stayed calm and did not waver.

He slid his gun back into the holster.

I leaned forward. "You are here because God put you here, and he has put you to a test. Will you abide in God or in the will of a man—your ultimate boss, President Ceaușescu, who requires you to worship him? God has given you free will to choose."

His eyes softened. God's Word was reaching him. My heart thumped even faster, and my confidence rose. God's love for the world—and specifically for my killer—throbbed in my heart. The Lord's authority over all earthly thrones, dominions, and powers strengthened me.

"The truth is that we have all been corrupted and gone away from God."

He nodded.

"We all are sinners, and our sin has determined our future. Hebrews 9:27 says, 'People are destined to die once, and after that to face judgment.'"

His mouth fell slightly open, and his hands relaxed at his side.

I continued, "'Anyone whose name was not found written in the book of life was thrown into the lake of fire'—that's Revelation 20:15."

"The Judgment Day," I added.

He frowned and straightened. The man with eyes full of hate reappeared. He reached into his coat and touched the weapon, as if to remind himself—and me—that at any moment, he could draw the gun and put a quick end to my testimony.

In my spirit I heard the direction clearly: *Virginia, now is not the time for you to trust your own words; you must stick to Scripture.*

I straightened and met his eyes again. "But the good news is that God has prepared a way out for every one of us through the sacrifice of Jesus Christ on the cross: 'For God so loved the world that he gave his one and only Son, that whoever believes in him shall not perish but have eternal life—John 3:16.'"

God's words flowed like refreshing water through me and showered the man. He appeared smaller and more peaceful than the large, angry man who strode into my office moments ago. Chills tingled from the back of my neck to my fingertips. "'Believe in the Lord Jesus, and you will be saved'—Acts 16:31."

His brown eyes remained locked on mine, attentive, searching.

"I needed once and you need now to be born again by the Spirit of God," I told him. "Accept Jesus Christ as your Lord and Savior so that you can obtain the forgiveness of your sins, otherwise you will be condemned on the Day of Judgment."

I reached forward and touched his folded hands. "You

must make the right choice today. God has given you this golden opportunity, so please take it. Jesus said, 'I am the way and the truth and the life. No one comes to the Father except through me'—John 14:6."

I stared deeply into his eyes. So deeply, that I could almost see a change taking place.

This trained killer must have carried out dozens of assignments such as the one that brought him to my office today, but when confronted by the power of God's Word, his heart melted. God's Word was saving us both!

He brought his hand to his forehead. "You are right. The people who sent me here are crazy. I do need Christ."

"Would you like to invite Christ into your heart?"

"Yes," he whispered.

"Repeat after me, 'Jesus Christ, I am a sinner. I accept you as my Lord and Savior.'"

He said the words, then rose. "You are doing what is right. These people are crazy." He opened my door, and before leaving said, "I will come to your church as a secret brother in Christ. I will worship your powerful God."

And with that, my killer walked away saved—a brother in Christ—but that didn't change the fact that the dictator's regime had issued a contract on my life.

This was God's battle and I was his tool! I rejoiced.

This man had defied direct orders to kill me. Surely this would not be the end of it.

What would happen to him?

To me?

CHAPTER 14

*You see these dictators on their pedestals, surrounded by
the bayonets of their soldiers and the truncheons of their
police . . . yet in their hearts there is unspoken fear.
They are afraid of words and thoughts: words spoken
abroad, thoughts stirring at home—all the more powerful
because forbidden—terrify them. A little mouse of thought
appears in the room, and even the mightiest potentates
are thrown into panic.*

—WINSTON CHURCHILL

EARLY THE NEXT MORNING, I fixed my coffee, read my Bible,
and waited for the alarm to wake up the girls. After a quick
breakfast, we got ready to head off for school and work.

As we opened the door, two armed police officers blocked
our exit, and several others surrounded our house. I tried to
remain calm so as not to upset the girls, who were still a bit
rattled from the other night.

"Good morning, officers," I said as politely as possible.
"What is going on?"

"You are under house arrest," one of the two men blocking the door barked. "You and your girls cannot leave this
house. Understood?"

"Why?" I asked.

"Back in the house!" he said, shoving me back into the entry hall. "And stay there!"

Enraged, I slammed the door shut and ran to the phone. Once again, it was dead.

"Girls, go to your room and play," I said, ushering Andreea and Anca down the hall.

"Mommy, who is that man?" Anca asked. "Why won't he let us go outside?"

"I'll explain later," I said. "I promise. For now, I just need you to stay in your room, okay?"

With the girls tucked safely away in their room, I frantically paced the hall. I felt alone and trapped. Even worse, Radu was once again out of town and wouldn't be returning for at least three more weeks—that is, if he didn't decide to take a detour on his way home to play the ponies again. I was exasperated. *That man is never around when his family needs him!* Of course, it wasn't all his fault. The *Securitate* obviously knew Radu's work schedule. Why else would they always schedule their little "visits" when he was out of town and I was alone with the girls? With no one else to turn to, I turned to the one I knew would *always* be there.

Lord, it's just us; only us, I prayed. *I cannot talk with anyone. I cannot alert Radu or anyone else. Lord, you are our only protector. Show your power and provision to me and my girls. Give me your peace and guidance and the courage to stand tall for my girls. And please, Lord, have mercy on those policemen guarding us.*

One day slowly melted into the next. I tried not to worry about our food supply. Instead, I focused on turning my worries over to God. And I learned to wait. Sometimes waiting is long and tiresome; I learned that, too. Strangely enough, having grown up with very little food prepared me "for such a time as this" (Esther 4:14). My girls, however, were a different story. Every day, they grew more and more impatient, constantly barraging me with questions.

"Why can't we go outside?"

"When can we go back to school?"

"Why is our house being guarded by policemen?"

"Why doesn't our phone work?"

It was hard for me to explain.

"Do you remember when I told you that your teacher was afraid people would be angry with her if they knew she believed in God? Well, the men outside are angry at us because we believe in God, and they don't want us to go out and tell other people about him."

It wasn't an ideal explanation, but it helped, though only for a short while.

Some days all I could do was quiet their cries as they stared through the window at the world going on around them while armed *Securitate* lurked about our front yard, laughing, smoking cigarettes, and stomping out the butts on the lawn.

Other times, the sheer injustice of my punishment and its impact on them made them angry.

"It isn't fair!" Andreea would complain. "What if they fail us in school because we're not there?"

"I'll never get caught back up," Anca whined.

I did my best to reassure them. "Don't worry. I'm sure they'll let us out soon." But even I wasn't convinced. As the days turned into weeks, I tried to keep them occupied by playing games, but I could tell their hearts weren't in it.

If only the nanny could get through, I thought. I had seen Maria lurking across the street several times. We had even made eye contact once or twice through the curtains. But each time she tried to approach the house, the guards would turn her away. The last time she came by, I caught her eye just before she turned away and mimicked holding a phone up to my ear as if to say, "I'll call you as soon as I can." She nodded briefly, smiled politely at the guard, and left.

"Mommy, why won't the guard let Maria in?" Anca asked, watching the scene unfold from behind me.

"I don't know, sweetheart," I said. "Probably for the same reason they won't let us out. They are afraid of what we might say."

"But . . ."

"Please, no more questions this morning," I said, cutting her off briskly. She looked despondent. I kneeled down, kissed her cheek, smiled, and said, "Go get your sister and tell her it's time for breakfast, okay?"

"Okay, Mommy," she said, smiling.

The girls had both gotten very good at reading my moods, and often they took their emotional cues from me. *I have to be more careful around them,* I thought. *If I begin to lose heart, they will too.* I glared at the *Securitate* standing on the front walk, lighting another cigarette as he watched Maria walk away. *I will not let that happen!*

In an attempt to instill a sense of normalcy, each morning, the girls and I would dress for school and work and attempt to leave. And each morning, the officer guarding the door would force us back into the house, where we would settle in at the kitchen table and work on the girls' school lessons. If the *Securitate did* know Radu's schedule, which I had no doubt they did, we could be stuck here for several weeks—possibly even a month. It was bad enough the girls were being unjustly punished because of me; I would not have them held back a year in school as well.

On Sundays, we did Bible studies and sang worship songs together. It was important to me that the girls continue to worship God, not so much despite but *because of* our current situation. I wanted to make sure they knew that what was happening to us was not God's fault. That we were not being punished because of God, but because of the *Securitate*'s anger toward God and everyone who believed in him.

"They can keep us locked inside," I would tell them. "But they cannot keep God out!"

Then one morning, after almost two straight weeks of house arrest, I opened the door to go to work as usual. I was supposed to appear in court that day, so I assumed I would once again be turned back inside.

"Good morning, Officer," I said, politely. "If you don't mind, I am due in court this morning."

He looked down at me, sneered a bit, and then stepped

aside so I could pass. I was stunned. *Should I go get the girls?* I wondered. Fully expecting to spend another day doing lessons at the kitchen table, I had let them both sleep in a little this morning. I looked back at the front door, but I was hesitant to go back into the house, for fear that he would not let me leave again. *By the time I get the girls up and dressed, they might change their minds.* I walked as quickly as I could to the closest public phone I could find and called Maria. I told her to get over to the house as quickly as possible to look after the girls, and to call me right back if the *Securitate* did not let her in. Since she lived just a few doors down, I knew it would take her only a couple of minutes to get to the house. After nearly ten minutes had passed with no word from her, I assumed the *Securitate* had granted her access to the house and—knowing the girls were safe—quickly made my way over to the courthouse. *I wonder why they let me out today of all days.* Then I realized why.

It was the morning of the trial for Simion Barmus, the pastor of an Evangelical church in Bucharest, who was accused of storing and sharing Bibles that were printed in the United States, and in doing so, cooperating with the capitalists. Surely representatives from the American embassy, the Voice of America, and Radio Free Europe would all be in attendance at the trial. If I did not show up for the trial, they would know something was wrong. Ceaușescu was cruel, but he was not stupid. As soon as I set foot in that courtroom, anyone who had heard rumors that I was being held under house arrest would either think the rumors were false, or that

I had broken under the pressure and agreed to cooperate with the government.

When I arrived, my clients were almost as surprised to see me as I was to be there. With strength and clarity I could only attribute to God's intervention, as—thanks to the *Securitate*—I had not seen the case files for almost a month, I presented my argument. Unfortunately, I did not have all the documents I needed to complete my case. Figuring I had nothing to lose, I asked the judge for an extension.

"Your Honor, I would like to ask for some additional time to secure and present the remaining evidence," I stated calmly.

"Would the Counselor please approach the bench," he said sternly. "May I ask why you did not bring all the necessary documents with you today?" He was clearly angry. Frankly, so was I.

"Your Honor, my office was recently 'searched' by the police, and I have not had ample time to straighten up and reorganize all of my files." Part of me wished he had not called me to the bench so all those in attendance could have heard my excuse. Of course, he probably already knew why I was unprepared, which is precisely why he conducted our conversation in private.

"Very well," he said. "You have two weeks to produce the necessary evidence."

"Thank you, Your Honor," I replied. *Will the* Securitate *even let me go back to my office?* I wondered.

Back at the defendant's table, I spoke briefly with my client.

"I was interrogated," he whispered. "They wanted me to sign a complaint against you, but I told them *never!*"

Just then, one of the *Securitate* approached me. "You must follow us," he said gruffly.

"Thank you," I said to my client as I closed up my briefcase. "I'll see you in two weeks." At least I hoped I would.

As I followed the officer out of the courthouse, I started praying. *"Do not be far from me, for trouble is near and there is no one to help"* (Psalm 22:11). I was convinced that God heard me and that he alone held my life in his hands; that lifted my spirits immeasurably.

When we got to the corner, I desperately wanted to duck into the grocery store to buy some food, but the *Securitate* officer pushed me forward. "You are going home," he said, "not shopping. If you don't like it, I can take you to headquarters."

That was when I noticed that four other *Securitate* officers had joined us. Frustrated as I was, I couldn't help but smile that they felt it necessary to have five fully grown, heavily armed men guarding an eighty-seven-pound woman. Was I really that much of a physical threat?

When we got within a block of my house, the four additional officers who had joined us outside the courthouse peeled off, and just the original officer followed me to my door where yet another officer was posted.

"Thank you for the escort," I said politely. He just looked at me quizzically and departed.

Smiling at the officer standing guard, I opened the door and walked inside. I could hear the girls playing in their room, so I collapsed into a chair, exhausted. I wanted to cry, scream, kick, and scream some more, but the girls must have heard me come in, because they immediately rushed in.

"Mommy is home! Mommy is home!" They squealed, racing into my open arms.

I smiled and hugged them tight.

"Did you have a good time with Maria today?" I asked.

"Yes!" Anca replied. "We played all kinds of games."

"That's wonderful," I said, noticing Maria standing in the doorway. Still hugging the girls, I mouthed a quick but sincere *Thank you*. Clearly, God had sent me an angel in that woman.

"Come on," I said. "Let's have some lunch. Maria, you can go now, if you'd like. We should be fine."

"Shall I come back tomorrow?" she asked.

"We can certainly try," I said, laughing. I had no idea how long this little grace period would last. *For Simion's sake, hopefully long enough for me to get back into my office again,* I thought.

As the girls took their seats at the table, I scanned the mostly empty cabinets. I managed to scrape together a couple of cheese sandwiches on what was now rather stale bread.

Because there wasn't much left, I pretended I wasn't hungry and just had a glass of water. Drinking it, I found myself fighting back tears. I took a deep breath. I had to be strong for the girls.

Just then, the doorbell rang. I nearly jumped out of my own skin. We hadn't had a visitor in weeks.

"Doorbell, Mommy! Doorbell!" the girls squealed, dropping their sandwiches and racing toward the door. "Maybe it's Daddy!" Andreea said, reaching for the knob.

"Girls, wait!" I said sternly. "Let me open it." After all, I had no idea who was on the other side, and the *Securitate* had already sent one assassin to kill me. *Of course,* I smiled to myself, *that didn't go quite the way they'd planned.*

I opened the door to find Brother Neamtu, one of my clients, and his wife, Ana.

Brother Neamtu had been jailed for his faith, for teaching others to become lay pastors, and for sharing the gospel with his coworkers. I had visited him in jail while I was defending him. The charges against Neamtu were dismissed later by the court. He was released after spending six months in jail.

At the end of one of my jail visits, I prayed for Brother Neamtu, and the guard who was watching us burst into laughter. But then, as I continued praying, he stopped laughing and went stone still. As I left, I noticed his eyes were watering. *Another soul in need of Jesus,* I thought as I left the jail.

"Come in. Come in," I said, quickly ushering them inside and closing the door behind them. "How did you get past the guard?"

"He was having a cigarette out front, so we snuck along the side of the house. I don't think he saw us," Brother Neamtu replied.

For some reason, I found that hard to believe, but I was so grateful to have company, I decided not to question it.

I knew Brother Neamtu believed in angels. Perhaps one of them had distracted the guard. Either way, I was anxious to speak with him, so I sent the girls to play in their room and invited Brother Neamtu and his wife into the kitchen to talk.

"You look tired and worried, Sister Virginia," he said, looking into my eyes. I didn't doubt it. "Let me share with you something that helped me when I was in jail." Then he started to sing a song I hadn't heard before, and his wife joined him.

The song was about how trials and tribulations will come to us because the world hates Christ and it wants to destroy all who follow him. After several verses reminding us how Christ suffered for us so we could experience God's goodness, the song concludes with this powerful verse:

> *Tu catusele atunci le saruta.*
> *Rugator pentru cei ce le-au pus.*

> *Kiss the handcuffs that limit only your temporary freedom.*
> *Pray for your persecutors.*

Because, as the song points out, in this way, you will show them Christ, and one day you will reign with the Lord in glory.

It was so beautiful, I started to cry. Even the girls came out of their room when they heard it.

"You have to sing with us, sister," Brother Neamtu insisted.

"Yes, Mommy," Anca pleaded. "You have such a pretty voice."

"Please!" Andreea joined in, tugging at my sleeve.

"But I don't know the song," I said bashfully. "This is the first time I've heard it."

"It's okay," Brother Neamtu said. "We can teach you." With that, he and his wife led my girls and me back through the verses, and soon all of us were singing along together. I wondered if the officer standing guard could hear us. I hoped he could.

After we finished singing, we prayed as a group, and then Brother Neamtu and his wife left.

"Who were those people, Mommy?" Anca asked.

"They were angels," I said, smiling. And I believed it. Once again, God had made his presence known to me in my darkest hour. God had brought me to Brother Neamtu during his imprisonment, and now he had sent Brother Neamtu to me during mine. The lyrics to the song he sang first for and then with us were exactly what I needed to hear at that moment, and they further intensified the fire in me.

In the beginning, it was hard to sing this song without crying or sobbing, but soon the song gave me wings to fly outside of my house arrest and helped me to feel love and compassion for each *Securitate* officer, no matter their actions. It also gave me a new perspective to see myself as God sees me, peace that we are in God's hands, and faith to stop doubting and start believing. Whenever my doubts returned (and they did often), I would sing this song, and my doubts would vanish.

"We should sing this song more often," Anca told me one day. "Those *Securitate* need to hear it."

"Then maybe they'll understand that we don't hate them," Andreea added. "And you know what? Maybe they will accept Christ too! Who knows?"

From the mouths of babes. Amid all the anger and anxiety of being held captive, hearing my girls echo my own heart— to witness to those who were doing us harm—made my heart feel so full I feared it would burst.

*

Several days later, we received another unexpected visitor.

"Cousin Alin is here!" the girls squealed, welcoming in the tall, intelligent medical student from Bucharest who had entertained them many times before. Although we were not actually related, they had long considered him an adopted cousin, of sorts.

Alin was the middle child of one of my clients, Dr. Silviu Cioata from Ploieşti. Dr. Cioata was thrown in jail for talking with his patients about God and encouraging them to go to church. Dr. Cioata usually included a Bible verse with his patients' prescriptions, and then one day, one of his patients turned him in to the *Securitate*.

When I visited Dr. Cioata in jail, I was encouraged by his faith, his professionalism, and his incredible love for people. Eventually, the judge decided to release Dr. Cioata, deciding that the months he'd spent in jail had taught him to be loyal to the government.

Since Alin and his family were placed under house arrest while his father was in jail, he knew plenty of games, jokes, and tricks that he could share with my girls.

"Why don't you all play in here while I go get dinner started," I said. "Alin, you are more than welcome to join us."

"Thank you, Mrs. Virginia," he said graciously.

Heading into the kitchen, I thanked God for bringing Alin to help entertain the girls. They were starting to go a little stir crazy, so Alin's visit was exactly what the doctor ordered.

I opened the refrigerator, looked into the pantry, and tried to figure out a way to stretch what little I had left into a decent meal for four. It would be tricky, but I could do it. But for how much longer? *They must realize by now that they will never break our spirits. Is their only option now to try and starve us into submission?*

I fixed something simple for Alin and the girls, planning—once again—to forego dinner myself. When I returned to the living room, the girls and Alin were gone. Frantically scanning the room, I saw a slip of paper on the table.

Shaking, I set the food down and read the note. "We are going to play in Cişmigiu Park. Be back soon. Don't worry about us. Rest. You need it." It was signed, "Alin and the girls."

My first thought was that it was a trick. I ran to the girls' room, calling their names, but they did not answer. I looked everywhere for them—under their beds, in the closets, behind the sofa—everywhere. There was no question about it. They were gone. My mind started racing. *Why didn't Alin say something to me before he left? Why would he take the girls in the first place? What if the* Securitate *sent Alin here as a trap? What if they have my girls right now?*

I looked through the window; the uniformed police officer with his big gun and omnipresent cigarette was still there.

More questions whirled through my mind. *How did Alin get inside our house in the first place? And how did a young man and two little girls manage to walk right past the officer guarding the house to get to the park? How would they get back in?*

Frantic, I put my head down on the sofa and started to pray.

Please, Lord, keep my girls and Alin safe. Don't let any harm come to them. Watch over them, Lord, and bring them back home to me safely.

I reread the note. "Rest. You need it."

He was right. I did need to sleep. But how could I nap? Especially now. I took a deep breath and exhaled slowly. *There is nothing you can do, Virginia. The girls are in God's hands. Alin found a way in. He will find a way back. God will keep them all safe.*

Reluctantly, I lay down on the sofa and closed my eyes but to no avail. So I picked up a book and started reading. I must have dozed off, because when I awoke, it was starting to get dark out. I pulled the curtains aside and looked out the front window. The guard was still there. I craned my neck to look down the street in the direction of Cişmigiu Park, but there was no sign of Alin and the girls.

I went to the kitchen and tried to distract myself by taking stock of the few scraps of food we had left in the pantry. *We really need fresh milk and eggs,* I lamented. *And bread and cheese and meat . . .* I continued compiling a grocery list in my head.

Suddenly, the front door opened and I could hear my girls giggling with delight. "Girls!" I rushed into the living room and bent down to catch both of them up in my arms. I could smell the fresh air and sunshine in their hair.

"We had such a great time at Cişmigiu Park, Mommy," Andreea said. "Cousin Alin took us to the ice cream stand, and we had vanilla *and* chocolate ice cream!"

"I hope it doesn't spoil their dinner," Alin said sheepishly. Little did he know, that ice cream was probably the best meal they'd eaten in days.

"We had running competitions too," Anca chimed in. "And do you know what?"

"What?" I played along.

"We are both faster than Alin!" she squealed.

"And he took us out on the lake in a boat!" Anca continued.

"Really?" I asked, looking up at Alin.

"I hope you don't mind," he said. "They seemed to enjoy it."

"Of course I don't mind," I said, my eyes glazing over with tears.

"We saw my classmate Nadina and her parents there too," Andreea said excitedly.

I froze for just a moment. *How did they explain why they hadn't been in school for the past three weeks?*

"We just waved at them," Alin said, giving me a knowing look.

"Okay, girls. I'm glad you had such a good time. Now go wash up for dinner," I said, shooing them out of the room.

"Okay," Anca said. Then she paused briefly, looked at Alin, and said, "Alin, I'm sorry that man hurt your arm." Then she bounded out of the room.

"What is she talking about?" I asked.

Alin looked over my shoulder, making sure both girls were out of earshot before responding.

"The *Securitate* followed us when they realized I had taken the girls. On the way back to your house, one of them approached me, took me a few steps away from the girls, and threatened that if I ever returned here or took the girls out to play again, I would be ex-matriculated from medical school—or worse yet, I would disappear completely."

My heart leaped into my throat. "Oh, Alin, I am so sorry," I said. "I don't know what to say. You were so brave to come here, and it was so kind of you to take the girls to the park. This has been such a difficult experience for them. I can't thank you enough. And of course, I understand if you choose not to come back again. The girls will hold today in their hearts for a long time."

"You're most welcome, Mrs. Virginia," he said, smiling gently. "It is the least I could do considering everything you did for my father and my family. Besides, I remember how difficult it was being under house arrest as a child."

"By the way," I said, "something has been bothering me all afternoon—how did you ever manage to get past the policeman in the first place?"

"I just walked by him," Alin said matter-of-factly. "I don't think he even saw me. Actually, I came by several times before, and each time, he pointed his gun at me and demanded that I leave. But this time, he just didn't seem to see me going in, or us leaving, either." He put his hands up in disbelief. "I don't know how else to explain it."

Of course we both knew there was only one explanation.

I thanked him again for coming, and he assured me that his family, their church, and many of the other churches I had defended all over Romania were praying for us. "Be strong and courageous, Mrs. Virginia," he said. Then he hugged me and left.

That night, it was practically impossible to get the girls to settle down and go to sleep. All they wanted to do was talk about their big day at the park with Alin. When they finally did drift off, they did so with smiles on their faces. I couldn't remember the last time I had seen them both that happy. As I closed the door to their room, I felt tears streaming down my cheeks. I was so grateful—to Alin, for putting himself at great risk to bring my girls one brief afternoon of joy; to the churches that were praying for us and for our safety; and of course, to God for orchestrating all of it. That night I drifted off to sleep thanking God for his continued providence and praying for the strength to endure and to continue to show his love and kindness to my persecutors.

The next morning, when I glanced out the window, I saw not the same officer who had been standing guard for the past three weeks, but a new young man guarding us. I didn't know his name, but I prayed for him nonetheless. One particular verse came to mind as I fixed my coffee: *"If your enemy is hungry, give him food to eat; if he is thirsty, give him water to drink"* (Proverbs 25:21). So I opened the door and offered my coffee to the young man.

"Are you crazy, lady?" he asked, pushing the coffee away. "I can kill you at any moment, and you offer me coffee?"

"I know you can," I said, smiling. "I don't hate you for that. God loves you just as he loves me." The guard stared at me blankly.

"Get inside," he barked, pushing me back with his gun. I could have sworn, though, that for just a moment, his eyes changed, softened.

Taking a sip from the coffee cup, I smiled and went back inside. *He's thinking about it,* I mused. *I'll try again tomorrow.*

Heading into the fourth week of house arrest, things were starting to get desperate. We were already out of fresh fruit and vegetables, and the canned food was running low. That meant I had to be all the more creative in preparing food for the girls. I started slicing the bread paper thin and putting water in the milk and boiling it to make it last longer. I continued to pretend that I was not hungry myself so there would be more food for the girls. My faith was strong, but physically, I was starting to weaken.

Then things got worse. Sometimes in the morning, I would notice that small things were moved around by the *Securitate*. I tried to put everything back in the right place before the girls noticed, because I couldn't imagine what it would do to them, psychologically, to realize that even the prison of our home had been invaded while we slept.

As the days stretched on, our once-comfortable home started feeling smaller and smaller. Sometimes it was hard for me even to feel alive. Praying and reading the Bible helped. The girls played, invented new games, and sang to the Lord. Their songs invigorated my soul and gave me a reason to go on.

Somewhere along the way, we stopped looking outside and dreaming of a day when we could be out in the world again—working, going to school, worshiping with fellow believers, shopping, breathing, and just being free. It was painful to dream. Yet my soul refused to lose hope in the promise that God would provide for us.

Then one morning, all of the lulling sameness was interrupted by the doorbell. I opened the door to find an unfamiliar woman standing there. I invited her inside. She spoke only a little Romanian, and that with a funny accent. When she uncovered her head and took off her coat, I recognized her as the American ambassador's wife. I had met her at the embassy at the last Fourth of July reception.

"I am here to let you know that we at the American

embassy and in America care about you," she said. "I was sent here to make sure that you are all alive and well. The policeman outside didn't stop me or ask me anything. He might take me to jail as I leave, but everyone at the American embassy is watching." She took my hands in hers and looked deeply into my eyes. "We want you to know you are not alone. We will do whatever it takes to help you."

Glancing at her watch, she said, "I have to leave now." She put on her coat and covered her head. "Wish me luck," she said. "We love you." Though her words were filled with courage, I could not help but notice she was fighting back tears.

I closed the door after her and prayed that the Lord would protect her.

I prayed he would protect all of us.

CHAPTER 15

In the truest sense,
freedom cannot be bestowed;
it must be achieved.

—FRANKLIN D. ROOSEVELT

PRESIDENT CEAUȘESCU'S government worked in stealth mode, not only in relation to the Romanian citizenry, but also within the government itself. Even the *Securitate* and the American embassy didn't know what the government would do next. That may have been because the dictator himself didn't know.

All over Romania, Baptist, Pentecostal, and Evangelical churches held daily prayer meetings asking God for my family's release from house arrest. Naturally, that infuriated Ceaușescu. What seemed to worry him most, however, was that other attorneys would follow my example and take up the fight for freedom against him.

One morning, after weeks without a working telephone, we were awakened by the sound of ringing. Apparently, at some point while we slept, the *Securitate* had reconnected our phone.

Instinctively, I picked up the receiver, but before I could say hello, an unfamiliar voice stated, "You must come and pick up your passports and leave Romania."

My response was automatic. "I didn't apply for a passport." It was true. I hadn't.

Under Ceaușescu's regime, if someone applied for a passport to leave Romania, that person and his or her family would immediately be considered dissidents, enemies of the state, even enemy capitalist lovers. All of them would lose their jobs and homes; some would be jailed or even killed. *This must be some kind of trick,* I thought. *The government is trying to come up with some trumped-up charges so they can have an excuse to throw me in jail—or worse.*

"We have them almost ready for you," the voice continued. "Come on Monday at 10:00 a.m. to complete the paperwork. You must leave Romania. If you refuse, you will be killed."

Before I could respond, the line went dead. I was speechless. *They're going to arrest me on Monday.* I looked outside, and for the first time in months, I didn't see any armed officers guarding the house.

What was happening? The phone was back on. The armed guards were gone. Even if it was some kind of a trap, I was too excited at the prospect of actually leaving the house to care.

I hurried down the hall to wake up the girls.

"Girls, look outside. The policemen are gone!" I announced.

They quickly scrambled out of bed and over to the window to see for themselves.

"They *are* gone!" Anca shouted.

"Does this mean we can go outside?" Andreea asked.

"I think so," I said. "Hurry up and get dressed."

"Where should we go first?" Anca asked, riffling through her dresser to find a clean outfit.

I thought about that for a moment. It had been so long since we'd left the house, even the simplest trip would feel like a monumental event. There were, of course, a lot of places we needed to go—the grocery store, the butcher, my office. Then I realized what day it was, and our inaugural destination became obvious. "It's Sunday," I said. "Put on something nice. We are going to church."

"After church, can we go to the park?" Andreea asked.

"We'll see," I said. "Now hurry up and get dressed. We don't want to be late."

As the girls chattered excitedly about all the places they wanted to go after church, I headed back to my room to get dressed myself. *Thank you, Lord,* I prayed, *for your continued faithfulness.*

Just then, the front door opened, and a voice almost as foreign as the one I had heard on the phone that morning called out, "Virginia?"

Oh, my goodness. It was Radu.

"Girls!" I called down the hall. "Your dad is home!"

The girls bolted out of their bedroom like bulls out of a chute and flew into Radu's arms. "Daddy!" they cried.

"You missed it," Anca said.

"Missed what, sweetheart?" Radu asked.

"The police have been standing guard outside our house since you left," Anca explained excitedly. "They wouldn't let us out."

"We couldn't go to school or to the store or anything," Andreea said.

"We're almost out of food!" Anca piped in.

Radu looked up at me, lost. "What are they talking about?"

"After you left, the police showed up and ransacked the house, claiming to look for gold, guns, and American currency," I explained. "The next thing I knew, they cut the phone service off and put us all under house arrest." I motioned toward the front door. "They've had at least one officer posted at the door for the past month making sure nobody got in or out."

"But why?" he asked. "What did you do?"

Naturally, he blamed me.

"I didn't *do* anything," I said flatly.

"Mommy says the police were guarding our house so we couldn't go out and tell anybody about Jesus," Anca chimed in.

Radu's expression darkened.

"I thought someone followed me today. So this is all because of those clients you represent," he said accusingly. "Your church friends."

"Yes, Radu," I stated flatly. Clearly, he did not understand.

"You put the girls at risk," he said.

I was in no mood to argue with him.

"As you can see, the girls are just fine," I said. "And the police are gone. No doubt because *you* have returned."

His eyes darkened. "Are you saying this happened because I was gone?"

"No, Radu. I'm not." I sighed. I felt a headache coming on. "I don't want to get into this right now," I said. "Girls, go finish getting ready for church." As they scampered back down the hall, I stared at Radu. "Will you be joining us?"

"I just got home," he said.

"Well, we've been trapped here for a month," I shot back. "Whether you come or not, we're going." And with that, I turned and headed back into the bedroom to finish getting dressed. As frustrated as I was with Radu, I had to admit that after everything we had been through during the past four weeks, it was nice to have the whole family back together again. *If God can turn the heart of a trained assassin, surely he can reach Radu.*

Moments later, Radu appeared in the doorway.

"Virginia, I'm sorry," he said sheepishly. "I'm glad you and the girls are okay. Let me change my clothes and shave, and I'll come with you to church. We can talk about what happened later."

"Thank you, Radu," I said. Today was certainly full of surprises.

In all of the excitement, I had almost forgotten about the

mysterious phone call I'd received that morning. *How in the world will I explain* that *to Radu?* I wondered. I couldn't even explain it to myself.

*

Later that morning, we emerged from the house for the first time in almost a month—as a family. It felt so strange to be outside. While the girls rushed ahead, faces turned toward the sun, their hair blowing in the breeze, I instinctively held back. Stopping just a few feet outside the house, I looked all around, waiting for an armed guard to appear and force us back inside, but no one did.

"Are you okay?" Radu asked as I stood riveted to one spot.

I took one final glance around. "Yes," I said, feeling the warmth of the sun hit my cheeks. "I'm fine."

As we made our way to the church, we noticed several *Securitate* cars following us from a distance. The girls were happily oblivious, skipping ahead and chattering to each other. Radu looked paranoid and uncomfortable. And I fought the urge to start running.

If we can just make it inside the church, I thought, *everything will be okay.*

I was wrong. Things were better than okay. As soon as we got inside, the pastor and our fellow members all cheered for us. They hugged us, kissed us; some even had tears in their eyes. The contrast between this reception and the near-total isolation we had experienced for the past month was almost overwhelming. Even Radu seemed taken aback by all of it.

"You see?" I whispered to him. "We are like family to them."

The celebration was cut short by the pastor, who pulled me aside with a sense of urgency.

"The American embassy is on the phone," he said, leading me toward his office. "They want to speak with you right away."

I glanced over my shoulder at the crowd of people still surrounding Radu and the girls. Radu seemed to be in shock, but the girls were clearly loving every moment of their newfound celebrity.

When I picked up the phone, Michael Parmly was on the other end.

"I have wonderful news, Virginia. You are free!" he said, his voice filled with joy. "I am coming to see you this morning at church. Whatever you do, do not leave until I get there, okay?" Then the line went quiet.

I wasn't sure what to make of it. *You are free?* I'd never been free a day in my life. In spirit, of course, since I came to faith in Christ, but outside of that, I wasn't even sure I knew what the concept meant. *Maybe he was referring to the house arrest.*

Unsure of what to make of Michael's call, I went back to the sanctuary to meet Radu and the girls for the service, which, as it turns out, was dedicated to us. At one point, the pastor even invited the girls and me up front to sing the song that Brother Neamtu had taught us. By the time we finished singing, there was not a dry eye in the entire church. Then I spied someone at the back of the crowd, standing near the door. It was one of the *Securitate* guards who had been following us that morning. *Did he just wipe away a tear?* Yes. I was certain of it! Before I knew it, tears sprang to my own eyes. Suddenly, it was as though all of our suffering these past few weeks had a purpose. I reflected on the lyrics of that beautiful song:

> *Tu catusele atunci le saruta.*
> *Rugator pentru cei ce le-au pus.*

> *Kiss the handcuffs that limit only your temporary freedom.*
> *Pray for your persecutors.*

The day Brother Neamtu taught us that song, my girls told me we should sing it loudly enough for the *Securitate* to hear so that it could change their hearts. And now here we were.

As the weeping *Securitate* officer lowered his head— I hoped, in prayer—I quietly praised God and prayed that he would continue to work on the officer's soul. *Speak to all of them, Lord. Help them to see and understand the freedom you bring.*

At the end of the service, Michael Parmly and a few others from the American embassy arrived. Michael caught me up in his arms and swung me around, smiling and laughing. I had never seen him so happy. Then he looked me in the eyes and said, "America and President Reagan want you and your family to come to America. Please accept our political-refugee invitation." He was so excited, he packed the whole message into one breath.

I was speechless.

"What did you say?" Radu asked, stepping in between us.

"President Reagan has authorized us to grant your family political-refugee status," Michael repeated. "We have arranged for you to leave Romania at once."

Suddenly, it all made sense. *You are free. We have your passports waiting.* I stared at Michael blankly, unable to form words. He was serious. We really were leaving.

"We can't just leave," Radu broke in. "We don't even have passports. None of us are allowed to travel outside of Romania."

"Actually, Mr. Prodan, you do have passports," Michael explained. "We arranged for them last week while your wife and daughters were still under house arrest."

Radu looked at me. "Is he serious?"

"Yes," I managed. "I believe he is."

"Of course I am," Michael said, beaming. "Come back to my house with me. There are some people there who would like to meet you, and of course we have some paperwork for you to fill out. But yes, Mr. Prodan, I am serious. We are getting you and your family out of Romania immediately."

My head was spinning. All this time I thought we had been forgotten—cut off from the outside world—when in actuality, the outside world was working feverishly to help us. *Even President Reagan!* I looked at Radu, who stared back at me with a thousand questions reflected in his eyes—all of which I suspected I could answer with a single word—*God.*

*

When we arrived at Michael's house, Anca and Andreea were immediately whisked away by Michael's daughter, Bérengère, to play, and Radu and I were ushered into the living room, where two members of the United Kingdom's House of Lords (Parliament) and embassy officials from Israel, France, and Germany were waiting to meet with us.

"America is not the only country that is anxious to have you," Michael whispered. And he was right. One by one, each embassy official offered us political asylum.

"America is a young country with nowhere near as much history as ours," said one of the Parliament members, trying to tip the scales in favor of the United Kingdom. "Besides, America is so far away from Europe."

After the representatives had made their pitches, we respectfully thanked them for their desire to help us and told them we needed to talk about the decision as a family. No sooner had Michael ushered the others out of the room than we were joined by the American ambassador.

"And now," Michael said, smiling, "it is time for us to make *our* pitch."

"President Reagan has personally requested President Ceaușescu to allow your family to leave Romania within twenty-four hours," the ambassador informed us. "And he has already signed special political-asylum visas that will allow you to enter the United States."

"Here," Michael said, sliding a manila folder across the

table. "These are the immigration documents the American government requires. You will need to fill these out and return them to us within four days."

"You should also know that the *Securitate* is still interrogating your clients," the ambassador added. "We believe they are trying to force at least one of them to file a complaint against you so they can arrest you."

"So far, all of them have refused," Michael said, smiling.

"President Reagan is using the most-favored-nation status as a bargaining chip," the ambassador said. "He told Ceaușescu that if he wants to keep that status, he will let you and your family leave without any trouble."

My head continued to spin. There were so many things I wanted to say and so many questions I wanted to ask, but only Isaiah 43:4 came to my mind: *"Since you are precious and honored in my sight, and because I love you, I will give people in exchange for you, nations in exchange for your life."*

*

Back home, we prayed as a family, and then Radu and I sent the girls to the other room while we carefully considered our future.

"Do you really think we should leave?" Radu asked.

"I don't think we have any other choice," I said. "The *Securitate* has been interrogating all my clients trying to find someone they can bully or bribe into making a complaint against me. If they succeed, they could throw me in jail for years. You, too. Then who would take care of the girls?"

I could tell by his expression that he knew I was right.

"But what about the girls? Is this fair to them?" he questioned. "They would be leaving behind all their friends. It would be hard for them to start all over in another country."

"It's hard for them now, Radu!" I shot back. Then, realizing that the girls were only one room away, I lowered my voice to a whisper. "Or have you already forgotten that they have spent the past month locked up like prisoners in their own house? Even before the house arrest, their friends' parents started forbidding their children to play with them. People are afraid to associate with us, Radu," I stated emphatically.

I could sense he was weakening, but he was still uncertain.

"What about our families, Virginia? What would we tell them? Would our parents approve of this?"

I hadn't seen or heard from Stephen and Elena in years. They had never even met our daughters. The last time Elena had called, she had clearly communicated that they disapproved of my actions and that I was no longer considered part of their family. I knew she wanted the *Securitate* to hear her; I recognized the paralyzing fear in her voice. And even though Cassandra lived only a few miles away, she kept her distance out of fear too. The *Securitate* made certain that we were as isolated as possible.

"I haven't spoken to my family in ages," I said. "And you know your mother has never liked me. She'd probably be happy never to see me again." I chuckled.

Radu didn't dispute that. "But she would miss the girls," he said.

"Yes," I conceded. "But we might be able to come back and visit someday. Things could change." I leaned forward and met his gaze. "We have to leave here, Radu. It's our only chance."

Reflecting on Hebrews 11:8—"By faith Abraham, when called to go to a place he would later receive as his inheritance, obeyed and went, even though he did not know where he was going"—I prayed, *Lord, help! Give Radu the faith he needs.* Unlike Abraham, I felt sure I knew where we were going: America. We needed to get as far away from Romania—and Europe—as possible. Besides, everyone at the American embassy had been so kind. Some of them had even put their own safety at risk for me.

"You're right," Radu agreed. "I know you're right. So, I am assuming you want to go to America."

"Yes," I said with a smile, "America is the home of the free."

Radu chuckled and started leafing through the paperwork Michael had given us. "Their paperwork is easier, too. They require less documentation to immigrate than the Romanian government does for a simple passport."

The phone rang. I recognized the voice on the other end immediately. It was the *Securitate* agent in charge of my file—the one who had interrogated me at their headquarters several weeks ago.

"Mrs. Prodan, this is Banica Antonescu. You are to report to our office at 9:45 a.m. tomorrow about your passports. If you are late or you fail to show up, the passports will be destroyed and you and your family will be terminated." He said it all so casually, yet I had no doubt he was deathly serious. "You have been declared persona non grata by the Romanian government," he continued. "Consider yourself warned. 9:45 a.m. Do not be late." And with that, the phone went dead.

"Who was that?" Radu asked.

"It was the *Securitate*," I replied. "We are going to America."

First thing Monday morning, Radu and I showed up at the passport office, unsure as to whether we would be allowed to return home—or if we'd even survive the visit. We were immediately taken to separate rooms. My heart felt at peace, but my mind volleyed back and forth from thoughts of death to jail to freedom, over and over again.

We were both photographed, fingerprinted, and interrogated. The dictator himself called several times during the course of my interrogation. He was angry. I could hear him shouting over the phone. The terror on the *Securitate* agents' faces whenever he called made me almost feel sorry for them. Each time they stopped the interrogation to take a call from him, I took the opportunity to pray for them. In many ways, I realized, I was not the only person being bullied by the government here.

"Yes, sir!" the lead interrogator snapped, hanging up the phone. When he turned to face me, his face registered a peculiar mix of hostility and fear. "You are a disgrace to Romania!" he shouted. "We don't want you here. We don't want others to follow your example." I wondered if he had just been given this script over the phone. *Poor man. He is just a puppet.*

"Be happy we didn't charge you with being a spy for America," he barked. Then he leaned in and met my gaze. "You must never speak ill of Romania or our leader after your departure. Remember, he has eyes and ears everywhere." When I looked down, he lifted my chin to look me in the eyes. "And you still have friends and family here in Romania." A chill ran down my spine.

After hours of lectures, threats, and fear tactics, we were finally released with the promise that our passports would be ready "soon."

Strangely, I had become rather accustomed to the *Securitate*'s threats. In fact, I had experienced much worse. Radu, on the other hand, seemed shaken.

"You are right, Virginia," he said, sitting at the kitchen table later that day, looking defeated yet determined. "We have to leave here." He shook his head. "How can you remain so calm? Didn't they frighten you?"

"They used to," I responded. "Sometimes they still do. But I have learned to see the *Securitate* not as cruel and heartless enemies, but rather as fragile human beings who desperately need God's love in their lives." I sat down next to him. "I decided long ago to forgive them and to pray that God, who knows their hearts, will transform them. I believe that is part of God's mission for me—to love and pray for my enemies."

Radu looked puzzled. "I don't understand how you can do that. Especially after everything they have done to you."

"Trust me," I said. "Learning to love those cruel,

bloodthirsty, deceitful officers has been extremely difficult for me. I knew I could be salt and light for them, but *love* them?" I shook my head. "I could never do that by myself. Yet I knew I was called to do it. So every time they inflicted some pain or form of punishment on me, I would recite Matthew 5:44 to myself: 'But I tell you, love your enemies and pray for those who persecute you.'"

"And that worked?" he asked.

"Not at first," I admitted. "I struggled with it—a lot. And then one day, an officer in the interrogation room hit me so hard that my nose started to bleed, and instead of pain, I felt a powerful, loving force well up within me. Without even thinking, I looked up at this man and said, 'God loves you, and I love you too.' His hand, which had been raised to strike me again, stopped in midair, and his eyes began to water. He had to turn his face from me."

Radu sat transfixed.

"In that moment, I caught a glimpse of the awesome power of Christ's love. Because Christ's love conquers everything, he was able to instill in me a love for that man that I never could have felt on my own."

"You are an amazing woman, Virginia," Radu said.

"We serve an amazing God," I answered.

*

That night, we concentrated on completing the forms from the American embassy. We were able to answer all the questions except one: the city we wanted to live in. I decided to pray for God's guidance. *Lord, if you want us to go to America, you know exactly which city we should live in. Please make it clear to us.* I didn't pray this prayer just once, but many, many times that day.

The next morning, Michael came to the house and escorted us to the American embassy so we could hand in our paperwork.

"So," he said, "have you decided where you would like to live yet?"

"I have been praying about that," I confessed.

"Well, you still have a couple of days to decide," he said. "We can always fill in that final blank the day after tomorrow, when you come back to pick up your passports."

"We really do need to decide, Virginia," Radu said.

"Perhaps you should ask God again," Michael suggested, smiling.

"Don't worry," the secretary taking our paperwork said, her voice heavy with irony. "I'm sure if God doesn't answer you, the government will have a few suggestions."

The next day, I was still praying and waiting for God to give me an answer. After breakfast, the girls busied themselves by playing a game they had made up during our house arrest, running around the room and touching things according to colors. When Anca raced over to the table and touched the world map that Radu and I had been studying, I focused my gaze on America, praying that God would show me the city in that moment.

"Shhhh. Be quiet, girls," I said. Suddenly, I heard the name of the city in my heart.

"What's wrong, Mommy?" Andreea asked. And in that second, the name escaped me.

I looked at Radu. "I can't remember the name. It is the city where President Kennedy was killed."

"Dallas?" Radu said.

"Yes! Dallas, Texas!" I exclaimed. "That's where God wants us to live."

Radu shrugged. "Okay then. Dallas it is."

The next day, as I was walking into the consulate room, the same secretary welcomed me. She was holding a sheet of paper. "So, did God tell you the name of the city?" she asked.

"Yes," I replied. "Dallas, Texas."

"What?" she exclaimed, dropping the paper. I noticed she was trembling.

"Is something wrong?" I asked.

She gazed at me in disbelief. "Just in case you were unable to decide, our office made a recommendation—Dallas, Texas."

She and Radu exchanged shocked glances, while Michael and I merely smiled at each other and laughed.

"Well then, it looks like you're moving to Dallas," Michael said.

After signing the last of the forms, our next step was to buy our plane tickets and prepare our luggage. That wouldn't take long. The Communist government would not allow us to carry normal luggage. We could take only two handmade cloth bags, which we had to hand over to the government a week before our departure. We packed only a few articles of clothing and one pair of shoes each. Most everything else we gifted to our friends from church. All the rest of our possessions—including paintings, jewelry, furniture, and appliances—were confiscated by the government.

The day of our departure was set for November 1, 1988. According to our itinerary, we would first spend several weeks in Rome. From there, we'd be on our way to America. It was a bittersweet day. Though we were excited about going to America, it was hard saying good-bye to our friends from church. We tried to ease the pain by saying we would be back someday to visit, but deep inside, we all knew that day would likely never come—as long as Ceaușescu was in power.

Michael, Susan, and a few other friends from the American embassy met us at the airport. They wanted to make sure we were not stopped or arrested at the gate, and they stayed with us until we boarded the plane.

As we prepared to board, Susan gave me a big hug and whispered in my ear, "We have deposited some money for you at the Bank of America in Rome. Use it to buy whatever you need while you're there."

"Enjoy your time in Rome," Michael said. "Someone from the Department of State will contact you when you arrive." Then he gave me one final hug, winked at me, and said, "We will see you in America."

Our airplane from Bucharest to Rome was a small Soviet plane that shook violently and made a lot of noise. As soon as we took off, I started crying, and I couldn't stop. No matter how ruthless Ceauşescu and his *Securitate* were to me, Romania was my homeland, the only place I had ever known. I looked outside the window, trying to absorb every last image of Romania as we passed overhead and wondering whether I would ever be able to return. The pain seemed unbearable.

"What's wrong?" Radu asked.

I just looked at him, my eyes welling over with tears. Overcome with emotion, I uttered the first thought that came into my head. "I don't even speak English."

He just laughed. "You'll have to learn. The girls will too."

*

The airplane landed briefly in Tirana, Albania, to refuel. From there we flew on to Rome.

I was hopeful that our time in Rome might help me acclimate to capitalism and freedom, but I was wrong. Instead, the sheer diversity of the people, nationalities, and cultures we encountered overwhelmed me.

As we walked along Rome's crowded streets, I was appalled to see *Playboy* magazines hanging on racks everywhere. Some salespeople even offered the magazines to my girls. I was horrified. I was also appalled by the sight of so many young people openly doing drugs on the steps of the famous cathedrals, tossing their empty syringes on the ground like used tissues. *Even freedom has its ugly side,* I realized.

For the most part though, everything in Rome was majestic: the museums, the Colosseum, the parks, the shops. Everywhere we went, people in the streets would ask us what part of Italy we were from and what kind of dialect we were speaking. It was a whole new world for each of us, and it was beautiful.

The only thing that broke my heart was seeing all those magnificent cathedrals empty of worshipers. People just visited them as tourist attractions, taking pictures and then rushing off to visit another one. It seemed that even outside Romania, many people were spiritually poor, as the filthy magazines, lewd behavior, and empty cathedrals bore witness. When we stopped inside at one of the cathedrals, I took a few moments to pray for all the visitors to know Christ deeply.

Radu's nonchalant attitude toward all this concerned me. Nevertheless, I failed to see that our different values would contribute to the eventual downfall of our marriage.

During our stay, the American embassy also arranged for us to take a two-week training course to help us prepare for life in America. The girls got a real kick out of taking classes alongside Radu and me, and the two female teachers the American government provided were excellent. Of the four of us, Radu was the only one who spoke English, which proved both helpful and frustrating—especially since his study habits hadn't improved much from when he was in law school. While the girls were incredibly excited and continually peppered the teachers with questions, Radu seemed embarrassed by the fact that he was being taught by two women and spent much of his time either sulking or complaining.

Still, we learned a lot of valuable information. They covered everything from going to the grocery store (for some reason, we were never supposed to do this when hungry, which was puzzling, as I honestly couldn't remember a time when I *hadn't* gone to a food shop hungry), creating a budget, choosing an apartment, and finding a job, to applying for Social Security numbers and driver's licenses and enrolling the girls in school. We also watched videos that showed us how to avoid being scammed or taken advantage of by street vendors, salesmen, and taxi drivers. And we learned some key phrases, such as, "Howdy. Nice to meet you" and "I am new to Texas. Can you please help me?"

It was overwhelming but exhilarating.

We also received a crash course in American government. I especially enjoyed the presentation about the legal system. What a contrast to the Communist-run system I was accustomed to!

"Imagine, Radu, being considered innocent until proven guilty," I remarked one night as we—well, *I*—was studying. Guilt or innocence hardly seemed to matter in Romania. If the government didn't like you, they could pretty much do as they pleased. And if a law got in the way of their plans, the law was simply changed—or ignored.

I was also intrigued by what our instructors referred to as Miranda Rights. The fact that a defendant could refuse to speak with the police until he or she had an attorney present was magnificent. *How many of my clients have been forced or threatened into making false confessions before I was even able to meet with them? And how many were victims of judges looking the other way on established laws or prosecutors changing the charges in the middle of a trial to ensure their guilt?* It was mind boggling.

I knew that I wanted to continue practicing law in America, but my mind reeled with how much I would first have to learn. The systems were entirely different.

"You'll have to go through law school all over again," Radu cautioned. "*After* you learn English."

But I welcomed the challenge. The prospect of practicing law in a country where the accused had actual, legitimate, government-ensured and protected rights and where judges were neither appointed nor ruled in accordance with their loyalty to a dictator filled me with such excitement, I could barely sleep at night. So much of my life had been dedicated to seeking and defending the truth. *No wonder it was so difficult,* I mused. *I have been trying to defend truth in the wrong country.*

One evening in Rome turned out to be unforgettable for all of us. The US secretary of state was in town and invited us to have dinner with him. After dinner, his assistant took several pictures of us with him. "Your pictures will be in newspapers tomorrow!" he joyfully announced. "After you arrive in Dallas, look for an invitation to Washington, DC, to meet President Reagan," he added, shaking our hands before we said good-night.

The girls were giddy with excitement and kept me up late into the evening asking questions I was unable to answer but was anxious to find answers to myself: "What will our school be like?" "Will there be other Romanians in Dallas?" "Where will we live?" "Will we have a car?" "Where will you and Daddy work?" "How long do you think it will take to learn English?"

There was, however, one question I could answer for them. "Will we be able to talk about God in America?"

"Yes!"

*

Soon our time in Rome drew to a close, and we found our-selves back at Fiumicino Airport, where we boarded a jumbo jet for New York. The plane was large and luxurious, espe-cially compared to the old Soviet model we'd flown in ear-lier. When we landed in New York, I wasn't able to actually see the famous Statue of Liberty, but I definitely felt her spirit. The weight of almost three decades of Communist oppression finally lifted, and I practically floated down the jet bridge into the terminal.

"Is this Dallas, Mommy?" Anca asked, racing to look out of one of the terminal windows.

"No, sweetie. Not yet. This is New York. We still have one more flight to go."

As soon as we deplaned, we were met by a representative from the American embassy, who helped us go from one

terminal to another, leading us through crowds of travelers—
people who were free to go wherever they wanted. I looked
around at all the happy families toting their brightly colored
luggage; some were tanned from visiting warmer climates,
others were clearly sharing in the excitement and anticipation
of a grand adventure yet to come. *And not a single* Securitate
in sight.

"This is your gate," our representative said. "Your flight
to Dallas is scheduled to board in about twenty minutes. Is
there anything I can get you while you wait? Something to
eat or drink perhaps?"

I looked down to check with the girls, but they had
already darted over to the window to look at the plane, mar-
veling at its size.

"Daddy, come look!" Andreea called. Radu smiled and
went over to them, stooping down to point out the workers
loading the bags into the cargo hold. *I hope our luggage made
it here safely,* I thought. I would later find out that it hadn't.
When our things finally arrived in Dallas, the fabric bags
were torn and soaking wet, and our clothes were covered in
mold. The excellent condition of every other bag on the airport carousel left little doubt in our minds that the damage
had occurred in Romania.

I turned my gaze back to our escort. "No, thank you.
You have all done so much for us already." I could feel tears
beginning to sting the backs of my eyes. "We cannot possibly
thank you enough."

"It has been our privilege," she said, smiling. "Someone

will be waiting to meet you when you land to take you to your hotel and help you get settled. Also, we have set up a bank account for you to help get you started, and we have secured a two-bedroom apartment for you close to the school where your girls have been enrolled. Your escort will help you with all of this when you arrive."

I was so overcome with gratitude, I could barely respond, so I simply offered her a hug and murmured a sincere, "Thank you."

Thank you, Lord. Thank you.

It was evening when the plane began its final approach into Dallas. I sat beside the window and couldn't take my eyes off all the lights of the city. I watched the traffic rush past as we got close enough to see it, and deep within, I knew that I was catching my first glimpses of our new home.

As I prayed for our future in Dallas, Proverbs 30:7-9 came to my mind:

> Two things I ask of you, LORD;
>> do not refuse me before I die:
> Keep falsehood and lies far from me;
>> give me neither poverty nor riches,
>> but give me only my daily bread.
> Otherwise, I may have too much and disown you
>> and say, "Who is the LORD?"
> Or I may become poor and steal,
>> and so dishonor the name of my God.

The heart of those verses became my prayer: *Lord, give me neither poverty nor riches, but give me only my daily bread!* God had answered that prayer many times for me before, and I had no doubt he would always remain faithful to his Word.

As the wheels of our plane touched the ground in our new home, I leaned my head back, closed my eyes, and took a deep breath. My long and tumultuous journey had finally come to an end. A new and exciting journey was about to begin.

EPILOGUE

Dallas, Texas

2010

IT WAS A TYPICAL SUMMER DAY in Dallas as I drove to my office.

Perfect, I thought. *Ninety-degree heat and a traffic jam.*

When I finally got to my building, I parked in the underground garage and took the elevator to the third floor. The air-conditioning felt wonderful. At the door to my office, Cassie, my assistant, welcomed me.

"Good morning, Virginia," she said, walking beside me and handing me a cup of coffee. "We have a busy day today. I'm almost done organizing those files for your conference call and Skype interview this morning, and I'm working on two more for the afternoon. Also, the leader of the women's club just called to remind you of your speech at seven o'clock."

"Great," I responded. "What time is my first appointment?"

"Eleven fifteen."

"Thank you, Cassie," I said, opening the door to my office.

I settled in at my desk and began looking over my notes. A Swedish family wanted to file for asylum in America. The family wanted to homeschool their children, which is forbidden in their country. According to their country's law, if they refused to send their children to public school, they would lose their parental rights. Unwilling to bend, the parents refused, started homeschooling their kids anyway, got in trouble with the government, fled to America, and were now afraid to return home.

As I was reviewing their file, I heard a soft knock on my door. *Must be eleven fifteen,* I thought.

Cassie stuck her head around the door. "Ms. Prodan, your appointment is here."

"Thank you, Cassie. Please let him in."

"Okay," then she paused briefly and asked, "I am taking an hour lunch today. Is that okay?"

"Yes, of course," I told her.

Cassie then ushered the man inside my office and closed the door.

Facing me was a broad, muscular man with dark brown eyes, large shoulders, and a shock of white hair.

"Hello," he said. "My name is Michael Taut."

"Yes. We spoke over the phone. Please sit down," I said, reaching out to shake his hand. "Did you have any problem finding my office?"

"No," he responded. I watched as he placed his file on the table in front of him, nervously rubbed his hands, and looked around the office.

"Are you okay?" I asked. "Can I get you something? Water or Coke?"

"No. I am fine." He rubbed his hands again. "I don't know where to start." His eyes continued to dart around my office.

"Don't worry," I said warmly, trying to set him at ease. "Just say what you have on your mind."

He swallowed deeply and began. "As I mentioned on the phone, my son is a pastor in Fort Worth. The church offered him a job, and he and his wife moved here a year ago." He paused for a second. I noticed he had a slight Romanian accent. "My daughter-in-law is pregnant, and my son took her to the hospital this morning. She is going to have a baby today."

"Congratulations!" I said, smiling brightly. "I wondered why your son was not here with you."

Michael rubbed his hands together yet again and continued. "At the time my son was hired, his congregation was meeting inside the big Presbyterian church. Two years ago, my son's church purchased land, and finally, six months after my son got here, his church started to build. The church had secured all the required government authorizations and inspections, but now the government is suing them. Here are the papers," he said, handing me the file.

I glanced at the documents. "I might have to visit his church, talk with your son, and see everything there before I contact the government, so I can be prepared to respond to any of their questions."

He pulled out his iPhone and began typing something, then continued, "My son felt that the city government singled them out. Every other building around them received approval and is approved to open next week."

His phone vibrated softly in his hand. He looked down. "My son will be happy to show you the church building and talk with you this Friday if you can make it."

"Friday at two o'clock is fine with me," I responded. "Did your son have any problems with the authorizations before?"

"No."

"Interesting." I changed tack slightly. "So what is the situation with your daughter? You mentioned on the phone that she is a member of a Christian club at Vanderbilt and that she needs my help. I know that a few years ago, the club lost their status with Vanderbilt for limiting their board only to Christians. They were on probation for a while, I believe, and now," I continued, pulling his daughter's file out of the stack, "the university is requiring the club to accept non-Christians as board members—is that right?"

"Yes," he said, nodding.

"I would like to talk with your daughter about this. When is she coming back home?"

"Next weekend," he replied. "I'm sure she would love to come to your office the following Monday."

I checked my schedule. "Perfect. Monday at nine o'clock. You know, my daughter went to Vanderbilt, and she never experienced anything like this. I suppose things change," I said, sighing.

I looked up and noticed Michael's eyes glued to the picture of my children on the table behind me.

"You have *three* children?" he asked, rubbing his forehead. "I remember only the girls."

I froze. *Did I hear him correctly?* My mind began to race. *What did he mean by that? How would he know about my girls?* My son, Emanuel, had not been born until after we moved to America. *If he knew only my girls,* I reasoned, *he must have known them . . . in Romania.*

My pulse started to quicken. *Something about this man frightens me.* Suddenly, I realized that everyone, including Cassie, had gone to lunch. "Do you have any more questions?" I asked, standing up.

Michael cast his gaze down at the floor and rubbed his hands. "Virginia, do you remember me?"

My blood chilled at the familiarity of him using my first name. *Who is this man?*

As he reached into his pocket, I readied myself to make a run for the door. Then he produced a small photo ID card and held it up, his thumb covering everything but the photo. "Virginia, do you recognize this person?"

I stared at him blankly. *What is this?*

"Look at the picture, please," he implored, holding the card closer.

I leaned forward slightly and took a good look, and my heart all but stopped. *This cannot be possible.* I looked again. *No. It can't be!*

"I am the *Securitate* agent who was sent to kill you in your office many years ago in Romania. This is my *Securitate* ID." Michael moved his thumb so I could see the rest of the card.

I took an instinctive step backward. I felt blood rush to my head. I swallowed a scream. I wanted to run. But instead

I prayed, *"Come quickly to help me, my Lord and my Savior"* (Psalm 38:22) and politely responded, "You have changed a lot," nodding at his whitened hair.

"Oh, yes, I have changed," he said, a small laugh escaping his lips. "It's true, I have gained some weight, and my hair is almost white. But those are not the only changes." He caught my gaze. "I don't kill people anymore," he continued. "I bring them to life. I am a pastor."

"You are a pastor?" I said, stunned. *Is this one of his new tricks?* I clamped my shaking hands together. *Is he here to really finish his job? Lord Jesus!*

"Yes," he replied. "Immediately after the revolution, I enrolled in the theological seminary in Bucharest. I have been a pastor for almost twenty years, and our church is still growing. Ten years ago we bought land outside of Bucharest and moved our church there. We even built a Christian school for students from kindergarten through twelfth grade." Suddenly Michael pulled something from his pocket. Terror banged against my chest like a courtroom gavel. My legs shook. I could hear my heart.

It was just his phone.

"Here are some pictures," he said, handing me the iPhone.

I began swiping through the images, still in disbelief and shock. "The church is big indeed," I finally said. "What a great sanctuary, and look at those classrooms! I am so impressed." *Is this real? Is it even possible?* I looked up and met his gaze. I noticed his eyes were glazed over with tears. "God is so good," I managed to choke out as I handed him back his phone.

"My wife is here with me in Fort Worth," he added, tucking the phone back into his pocket. "She is here to help with our first grandbaby. We have three children too, like you," he continued. "Our other son is back in Romania, studying to become an attorney." He showed me another photograph on his phone. "Here is his picture."

I stifled a gasp as I looked at the picture. The resemblance was uncanny. "He looks so much like you," I exclaimed. "This is just how I remember you from Romania." Again fear overwhelmed me as the photo brought back memories of that first meeting. I forced myself to recall the peace of God that had filled me and led me to share the gospel with my assassin all those years ago.

I paused for a moment to let the weight of everything that was happening sink in. *I cannot believe this is the same man who was sent to kill me. He really did come to Christ that day. And look what it has led to—a church, a Christian school, and a son who is a pastor! Lord, you are amazing!*

"We also have a granddaughter! They named her Virginia," Michael announced, beaming. Tears went down his cheeks.

My heart caught in my throat, and tears began streaming down my cheeks. "Oh, Michael, that is so beautiful!"

He wiped the tears from his own face and then smiled brightly.

"Michael, we have to celebrate!" I exclaimed. "I will take you to lunch. I know a great place. My treat. I want to hear everything about your family and your church."

"Thank you. I would love that," Michael responded.

As I gathered my purse, I reached over and grabbed my pen to leave a quick note for Cassie in the event that our lunch ran long—which I was hopeful it would.

As Michael and I walked out of my office, I stuck the note to Cassie's computer. It read quite simply, "I should be dead, but I am alive—and celebrating!"

A FINAL NOTE FROM THE AUTHOR

A LITTLE OVER A YEAR after we arrived in Dallas, Ceaușescu's regime collapsed.

On December 21, 1989, as he was delivering his annual "golden era" speech to the Romanian people, he was confronted by a revolt at the hands of a hostile crowd. Caught completely off guard, Ceaușescu lost control and was stunned into silence. The next day, his personal *Securitate* guard and pilot bundled both Nicolae and his wife, Elena, into a chopper and flew them out of Bucharest.

As soon as I heard the news, I immediately sprang into action and organized a public protest asking that no country offer either Nicolae or Elena Ceaușescu asylum, so that they would be forced to stand trial in Romania.

When television coverage of my protest went live, I began receiving threatening phone calls from the *Securitate*. The callers demanded that I stop speaking against Ceaușescu. Emboldened by my new freedom, I informed them that not only would I *not* stop, but if they called and threatened me again, I would contact the FBI. Needless to say, the calls stopped.

A few days later, I learned that the Romanian army had switched sides and joined the revolt and that Nicolae and Elena had been captured in Târgoviște, a city about fifty miles outside Bucharest.

On December 25, 1989, after a hasty (and private) trial, Nicolae and Elena Ceaușescu were executed by firing squad.

After Ceaușescu's death, I defended him in media interviews. Regardless of how cruel and unjust he was, I felt he deserved, like anyone else, a fair and deliberate trial. I understood why Ceaușescu's opponents felt the need to "rush to justice," as it were. After all, they couldn't risk the chance that he would regroup and regain power. Still, I firmly believe that every individual has the right to a fair trial.

Today, Ceaușescu's rule is but a bad memory, the grandiose palace he built for himself houses an elected parliament, and Romania stands as a democratic nation that boasts a stable and growing economy and solid international relations with the United States and most of Europe. Once more, Christianity is thriving! Many of the churches that struggled to survive under the Communist regime have been revitalized, new churches have been opened, and there are even Christian schools and radio stations throughout Romania preaching and sharing the gospel freely and openly.

While it still saddens me greatly that so many innocent people were ruthlessly persecuted for their faith, I do take great solace and joy in knowing that their courage and sacrifice was instrumental in bringing about the spiritual renaissance that continues to thrive in Romania today.

As for me, I graduated from Southern Methodist University Dedman School of Law and am currently a practicing attorney with my own law firm in Dallas, Texas, and an allied attorney with the Alliance Defending Freedom, continuing to fight for religious freedom here in the United States and across the globe.

Sadly, shortly after we arrived in Dallas, my marriage to Radu ended. The children are all grown up. Anca graduated from Southern Methodist University and is currently a counselor; Andreea graduated from Harvard Law School and is now an attorney; and Emanuel graduated from the US Air Force Academy and is currently a rescue pilot for the United States Air Force.

I remain forever grateful for the divine appointment God entrusted to me in my early years as a Christian—defending the persecuted in Romania and praying for the salvation of our enemies. That appointment was for a specific time.

I am also grateful for my new appointment—my current work for freedom in America. I pray that God will continue to open doors for me to be a champion for religious freedom and a witness of his unending love and grace to many.

I have learned so much through my experiences.

- Freedom is precious to those who don't have it.
- If the truth lives within me, lies cannot overpower me.

- If my soul is free, no power on earth can enslave me.
- If God gives me the victory, defeat is impossible.

I hope these lessons translate from my life today as an American and into yours, no matter where you live on this planet. My desire is that through reading my book and seeing how God used me to accomplish amazing things, you will realize God has a grand plan to use you as well, and I pray you will not put off doing what God is calling you to do. God assigns, provides, protects, and gives victory to those whom he calls. If this had not been true in my life, I would not be alive today to write this message.

You were created to thrive and to do great things through God's power, no matter your circumstances. I hope to meet you one day on our journey together to victory!

AFTERWORD

A Final Note from My Assassin

I GREW UP AS AN ENTHUSIASTIC youth Communist Party leader of my school and my small town. I distinguished myself by spying on and betraying many of my classmates, friends, relatives, and acquaintances and by secretly reporting them to the Communist Party headquarters.

Because of that, after graduation from high school, I was recruited to enter the police officer school in Bucharest. The government provided everything for me free of charge— a fully furnished house, clothes, luxurious vacations, money, women, and power.

After graduation from police school, I remained in Bucharest.

As a police officer, I was the best at spying and at placing false documents in people's homes or workplaces, then arresting and torturing them. While in my custody, they all either confessed or died.

Soon the *Securitate* recruited me, and after three years of intense special training, I was truly a ferocious criminal and a vicious killer.

I was proud of my job, and with every assignment I accomplished, I received more rewards and promotions, the highest being promoted to the rank of Assassin, where my job was to kill political dissidents, including innocent Christians and, of course, Virginia.

I remember the day my boss took me to the Romanian Communist Party Palace on a special assignment. I was at the top of my career. After all, I had been granted the great honor of being in the same room with our leader, Nicolae Ceaușescu.

My boss told me that Ceaușescu was preparing to go on a long international trip that day, so I was overwhelmed that he still had time to meet with us. My boss approached Ceaușescu and spoke with him, while I stood a bit back. But I remember seeing the intense hate in Ceaușescu's eyes as my boss pronounced Virginia's name and the sinister smile on his lips as he imagined Virginia's death at my hands.

When Ceaușescu looked at me and nodded, I felt proud to be able to serve him. I knew that if I completed this assignment successfully, I might be promoted to Ceaușescu's chief headquarters officer. It would have been the greatest possible honor I could receive.

When I entered Virginia's office that afternoon, I felt alive—ready to kill her and ready to move up in my career. I was a man empowered to commit unthinkable atrocities upon people. But then God, in his amazing love, sent me to her office. My intention was to kill Virginia, but God's intention was to breathe life into me through her.

As I followed Virginia into her office, I thought first about strangling her. But then I decided it would be more enjoyable to frighten her by showing her my gun. I watched Virginia's reaction ecstatically. She was scared; I could read it on her face. Then as Virginia calmly shared the gospel with me, *I* was the one who was frightened—frightened of the peace and the power that came from such a petite person, who could not have weighed more than one hundred pounds.

And before I knew what happened, I was overwhelmed by the love embedded in every word that Virginia said. I don't know how she did it, but she made me want *her* God to be *my* God. Then she prayed for me. Nobody had ever done that before, and I considered that a much undeserved "reward."

I realized that not only was I a cruel, dangerous, and irrational man, but I was also a dead man. I was a man without God, one who loved only himself and possibly the dictator and power.

After I left Virginia's office, I started crying and thanking God for loving me. I cried so hard, I could barely see. I lost control of my car and woke up in the hospital. Later, I realized my boss assumed that I had been unable to accomplish my mission of killing Virginia because of the accident. I didn't correct him.

After the revolution, I decided to enroll in seminary to become a pastor. Since I had left Virginia's office that day after accepting Christ, it was all I thought about and all I wanted to do.

I heard about Virginia's emigration to America through a few pastor friends, and then I found Virginia's website. I searched her name every month, and eventually I realized that she was too important in my life not to go see her. Plus, I wanted Virginia to know that God used her to change my path and that I was indeed a new man who was now serving the God she introduced me to.

Recently, Romania has begun indicting former members of the secret police for atrocities committed against dissidents during Ceaușescu's reign, and I do not know when my own time will come. I know what I did, and I have to live daily with my past, but I also know that my future lies in Christ. God, in his mercy and love, forgives us. But when most people hear the name *Securitate*, they don't want to offer forgiveness. Virginia's forgiveness when I came to see her rejuvenated my soul.

The emotions that crossed Virginia's face when she recognized my *Securitate* ID made me realize what a monster I had been, but I had never forgotten her faith and her love for all people—even vicious killers like me. I wondered many times if I could live like Virginia—for Christ—no matter the circumstances. Before I went to see her in Dallas, I listened to Virginia's speeches on the Internet, and she always spoke about the day I came to her office in Bucharest without hate and without anger, but instead as God's way of bringing me to Christ.

When she recognized me and took me to lunch, I became convinced that I *am* Virginia's brother in Christ. No matter what happens to me, I will treasure that memory and extend to others—even those who may persecute me—the same love and forgiveness she has shown to me. It is hard to believe that one day Jesus will say to all of us, "Come, you who are blessed by my Father; take your inheritance, the kingdom prepared for you since the creation of the world" (Matthew 25:34).

If I *am* indicted in Romania, I can only hope that by the grace of God, Virginia's testimony will save my life—once again.

Michael

Q & A: AN INTERVIEW WITH VIRGINIA PRODAN

In the book, you drop several hints that Cassandra may have been more to you than just your aunt. Was Cassandra actually your birth mother?

Yes, she was. It wasn't until many years later—when I was in my thirties—that a close relative finally told me the truth. Unfortunately, by that time, Cassandra had already passed away.

Did you ever find out who your birth father was?

Yes, as a matter of fact I did (from the same relative). It was John, the gentleman who came to Cassandra's house while I was living there.

What happened? Why did Stephen and Elena raise you?

It turns out that John and Cassandra were close friends for years, and over time, he fell in love with her. Unfortunately, he was too shy to tell her. During their friendship, Cassandra spent a great deal of time taking care of her ailing parents, and before they died, she promised them she would take care of her two siblings, George and Elena (yes, *that* Elena).

Needless to say, for a young woman with two younger siblings to support, marriage was the furthest thing from her mind. Eventually frustrated by her lack of romantic interest in him, one night John forced himself on Cassandra, somehow believing it would bring them closer together. Instead, Cassandra broke up with him. She never reported him, but as revenge, she also never told him she was pregnant.

Four months later, Elena, who had recently separated from her husband, Stephen, arrived in Bucharest intending to stay at Cassandra's house. Now, back then in Romania, having a child out of wedlock was a source of great shame. So the sisters developed a plan—Elena would stay in Bucharest while Cassandra moved to the small town of Giurgiu to conceal her pregnancy until the baby was born. When I finally arrived, Elena declared me as her daughter at the city hall birth-registration office. That same afternoon, Cassandra returned home to Bucharest, and Elena returned home to Stephen with me, explaining that she had been pregnant when she left him. He was so happy to have Elena back, he didn't even mind that his new daughter had red hair and freckles.

Have you had any contact with Stephen and Elena since moving to the United States?
Six months after I arrived in Texas, I received news that both Stephen and Elena were very sick and in need of medication, so I immediately sent them the medicine they needed. Years later, I learned that Elena and Stephen never received

the medicine I sent. It turns out Ceaușescu had confiscated everything, and unfortunately, both of them died.

If Ceaușescu was so intent on persecuting Christians, why did his courts allow you not only to try their cases, but to win so many of them?

At first they didn't pay too much attention to me because I was only a woman—which to them meant someone weak with no voice. But as 1 Corinthians 1:27 says, "God chose the weak things of the world to shame the strong." Also, Ceaușescu wanted to show America and the West that there was indeed justice in Romania, and since Radio Free Europe and the Voice of America, who reported back to the States and Western Europe daily, were often present in the courtrooms where I filed and argued my cases, Ceaușescu couldn't risk the bad publicity that would result if I lost those cases. Of course, Ceaușescu's act was just a front. In reality, Christians were being persecuted all over Romania, and the laws protecting them were extremely obscure and changed constantly, usually in Ceaușescu's favor. I was able to win many of my cases because I was familiar with laws that Ceaușescu and the courts wrongly assumed nobody would ever cite.

What was the biggest challenge you faced starting over in America?

As a single mother, my biggest challenge was trying to balance raising three kids, working, going to law school, and rebuilding my professional life. But God was faithful, and his hand was with me every step of the way.

We are very lucky to live in a country that supports religious freedom. What would you like people in America to understand about religious persecution in other countries?
First, that freedom is a gift from God, and it is so precious to those who don't have it. That is why it is our responsibility to stand up and protect that freedom if someone ever tries to take it away from us. And second, that we need to fear God, not man. It is an honor to suffer for Christ—and loving him above all else is the only way we can win over the souls of those who persecute us.

Even my own persecution was limited in time and in action by God. He never gave my enemies the power to kill me. In fact, with every attack, God displayed his protection, timing, and grace—not only in my life, but the life of a nation and its people under a cruel dictator. It is easy to look back now and see it. But while it was happening, it took faith to step up and to go on.

Fortunately, God never stops teaching us and preparing us for more.

Have you returned to Romania since those dark days?
Yes, I went back in 1998 with a television crew from Dallas to visit some of the churches I had defended.

Were the churches still struggling?
No. In fact, many of the churches that I defended were flourishing! They had been spaciously expanded, each Sunday school class had Bibles and hymnbooks openly displayed,

and no one needed to fear serving jail time. In addition, we were free to speak with church members without worrying about whether or not any of them were spies. And we learned that some of the *Securitate* who had followed me were faithful members of those churches!

We also visited the Bucharest Theological Seminary, which used to have no more than two students as future priests—and they had to be members of the Communist Party. By 1998, the seminary was accepting between fifty and one hundred real ministerial candidates each year, and several other cities in Romania were planning to build their own theological seminaries.

Did you get to meet with any of your old law associates?
Yes. We actually filmed in the same courtrooms where I argued my cases, and many of the same judges and prosecutors were still there but with completely different attitudes. I could still remember the disgust on some judges' faces when they had to deal with me back in the day, but when I returned, they were all very polite and anxious to help. Of course, some were too embarrassed to show up, and a few simply extended a quick handshake and then left. But several wanted to talk more and invited me to their private offices, each of which had a Bible proudly displayed on the desk. What's more, they all assured me that nobody was arrested or jailed anymore for having a Bible, going to church, or watching a Christian movie at home. Some judges even told me that back when I was defending my clients in front of

them, they were scared for me and for my future and often wondered whether they would even see me the next day or if I would simply "disappear." They also told me that when the revolution finally came and Ceaușescu was killed, they ran to my church to hear the gospel. Now many of those judges, prosecutors, and lawyers are Christians, and they are serving Romanians *and* the Lord in freedom!

What was the most exciting change you saw during your visit to Romania?
Before we returned home to Dallas, I stopped at the biggest bookstore in Bucharest to buy some gifts for my kids, and it was there that I received one of my greatest gifts from God. The Bible was prominently displayed in the window and all over the store. Under Ceaușescu's regime, his pictures and books were virtually the *only* books to appear in the windows or on the shelves, as proof of the country's undying devotion to their dictator. At last his books and pictures were gone and the Bible he fought so hard to destroy was on display. It was so overwhelming that I knelt down in the middle of the bookstore and cried out joyfully to God, "Thank you, God, for appointing me, equipping me, and giving me victory in the job you gave me to defend freedom in Romania."

What do you feel God is appointing you to do next?
That day in the bookstore, I clearly heard God's voice within me saying, *Wherever you go and speak, encourage people to*

hear my call and to take the appointment that I have specifically prepared for them. That was God's message and his new assignment for me. Indeed, everything I accomplished in Romania was done by his appointment and his power. But that calling was for a specific time, and I can say gratefully that it is no longer needed in today's Romania. My new work is here in the land of the free and the home of the brave, and it is to help people understand that God has a specific, unique appointment for each of us to follow—one that can be accomplished only by his power working through us. If people take nothing else from my story, I hope they take this: You were created to do great things through God's power, no matter your circumstances. Listen for his calling, and when you hear it, embrace it and pursue it with all your heart. And do not be afraid, because as Luke 1:37 says, *nothing* is impossible with God.

ACKNOWLEDGMENTS

To MY CHILDREN, Anca, Andreea, and Emanuel—your love, strength, and support helped me remain so strong. I couldn't have survived the fire without you. I am proud to be your mom.

To God, who wrote each chapter in my life long before I scribed my story into this book.

To Jerry B. Jenkins, a rare talent and a sage advisor—with gratitude for your marvelous guidance and endless encouragement.

To my agent, Tawny Johnson, who from day one overwhelmingly knew that I have a remarkable story to share—for coming to Dallas to meet me and for your blissful, tenacious enthusiasm and boundless support.

To my editor, Carol Traver, senior acquisitions editor, Tyndale House Publishers—for your breathtaking love for my story and instant friendship; for your graceful, passionate, and professional guidance; and for your skillful assistance in polishing my manuscript.

To Jane Vogel, associate editor—for your important contribution to the final editing process.

To my publicist, Todd Starowitz, senior public relations manager for Tyndale House Publishers—for generously sharing your pearls of wisdom, invaluable suggestions, and insights and creating a rare and strategic vision for my book.

To Kristen Magnesen and Andrea Martin, Tyndale marketing and publicity team—for the ardent, exemplary work and for giving me the unique gift of glimpses into the publishing process of *Saving My Assassin*.

To each unsung hero who pressed the wet ink of your own journey into my life's pages—without you this book wouldn't have been written.

To my persecutors—for helping me trust God to teach me to love you as I never thought I could. I am a better person because of you.

To my readers—you inspired me! This one is for you. I trust the dangers and delights of my life adventures will inspire you, too. I am excited to hear from you and meet you all.

To my devoted speaking audience—I am indebted to you. Your encouragement and persistence made my days long and restless until I finally finished this book.

To my extended family—I am thankful for your love, prayers, Sunday lunches, and endless trips to airports, and for taking care of my dog, Holly.

ABOUT THE AUTHOR

VIRGINIA PRODAN is an international human rights attorney, an Allied Attorney with the Alliance Defending Freedom, and a sought-after speaker. Exiled from Romania since 1988, Virginia currently resides in Dallas, Texas. She has two daughters, Anca and Andreea, and a son, Emanuel. Visit her on Twitter @virginiaprodan, Facebook, and LinkedIn, and at http://www.virginiaprodanbooks.com and http://www.virginiaprodan.net/.

DISCUSSION QUESTIONS

1. The book opens with a young Virginia explaining how attending church under Communist rule "came at a great personal risk." To what lengths would you go to attend church under similar circumstances?

2. In chapter 2, Virginia talks about how she loves to escape through books, and she remarks at how much she has in common with Charlotte Bronte's classic heroine, *Jane Eyre*. What character from classic literature do you most closely identify with and why?

3. In chapter 3, Virginia's Uncle Carol tells her a chilling story about the little girl who lives next door. What do we learn from this story about Communism as well as about the short- and long-term psychological effect it has on those who live under its rule?

4. Chapter 5 opens with Virginia reciting the definition of *persona non grata*. How does the description compare with citizens' rights under a democracy? How would you define the ultimate goals of Communist Romania versus a democracy?

5. In chapter 6, we see both Virginia and Cassandra reacting very passionately to unexpected intrusions of certain men in their lives—Radu, for Virginia, and a stranger named John, for Cassandra. To what do you attribute the intensity of their reactions, and what does each woman's reaction reveal about her character?

6. What do you think motivated Elena to travel all the way to Bucharest to demand Virginia's return to Techirghiol?

7. In chapter 8, Virginia represents her first client in court. In what ways was her first trial a victory, and in what ways was it a defeat? What surprised you the most about Anton's case, and what does it teach us about the Romanian legal system under Ceaușescu?

8. In chapter 9, Virginia finally finds "the truth she had been looking for" her entire life. What are some of the lies she has encountered thus far in her journey, and how does this newfound truth help reconcile them?

9. In chapter 9, Constantin tells Virginia about the day the *Securitate* forced all the church members to choose between following Christ or going to jail (which under Communist rule could result in much worse punishment—even death), and asks her how she would prepare for such a day should it happen again. How would you prepare yourself for such a situation?

10. In chapter 10, we learn more about Ceaușescu's mistreatment of Christians and the church. Why do you think Ceaușescu was so opposed to Christianity?

What threat did organized religion pose to his rule
over Romania?

11. In chapter 10, it becomes clear that not only is Virginia
putting her own life at risk by defending fellow
Christians, she is also placing the lives of her children
at risk. How would you cope with such a harsh reality?

12. In chapter 11, we begin to see some of the ways
Ceaușescu's spies and secret police threatened
Christians on a daily basis. In what ways do Virginia's
clients' situations mirror those of the early Christians
in the Bible? What other parallels can be drawn
between Communist Romania and Christians living
in the first century?

13. Think about the encounter Virginia has with the little
boy on the street asking for bread. As he is led away by
his mother, Virginia wonders if the little boy will grow
up to be yet another defeated and obedient citizen.
Bearing in mind that Virginia was once a hungry child
herself, what characteristics did Virginia possess that
not only kept her from becoming a defeated, obedient
servant, but put her in a position to help others?

14. What do you think of Andreea's teacher's decision to
remain silent about her faith until after she retires? How
do you think you would have responded in her situation?

15. Back in chapter 9, Constantin asked Virginia how she
would prepare herself or the day she might have to
choose between her faith and her life. In chapter 12,

Virginia is faced with this very threat. How *has* Virginia prepared herself for such a moment?

16. In chapter 13, we finally see Virginia face her would-be-assassin. Put yourself in Virginia's shoes that day. How do you believe you would have responded to such a threat? What might you have said?

17. One of the major themes of Virginia's story is to constantly "pray for your enemies." We see Virginia do this several times throughout the book. Describe the impact Virginia's prayers and acts of kindness have on those she is praying for.

18. Upon their arrival in Rome, Virginia is appalled at the open display of adult magazines on the street and muses that "even freedom has its ugly side." What are some of the advantages and disadvantages of living in a free society?

19. Both Virginia and Michael decided to accept Christ after seeing firsthand the impact that faith in him had on others (Nestor for Virginia, and Virginia for Michael). What can you do as a believer to reflect Christ's power and love to others the way that Nestor and Virginia did?

20. Go back and revisit the brief epigraphs at the beginning of each chapter and discuss how each quote epitomizes a specific portion of Virginia's journey.

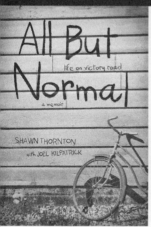

Love memoirs?

Find your next great read at MemoirAddict.com!

At Memoir Addict, we find ordinary people
with extraordinary stories.

Explore:

- updates on new releases
- additional stories from your favorite authors
- FREE first-chapter downloads
- discussion guides
- author videos and book trailers

- inspirational quotes to share on Pinterest, Twitter, and Facebook
- book reviews
- and so much more!

While you're there, check out our blog, featuring unique perspectives
on memoirs from all facets of the publishing industry. From authors
to acquisition directors to editors, we share our passion for story-
telling. You'll get an insider's look at the craft of shaping a story into
a captivating memoir.

Are you a memoir addict? Follow us on Twitter @MemoirAddict and
on Facebook for updates on your favorite authors, free e-book promotions, contests, and more!

Plus, visit BookClubHub.net to

- download free discussion guides
- get book club recommendations
- sign up for Tyndale's book club and e-newsletters

MemoirAddict.com:
ordinary people,
extraordinary
stories!

Online Discussion *guide*

Take *your* Tyndale reading
EXPERIENCE *to the* NEXT LEVEL

A FREE discussion guide for this book
is available at bookclubhub.net, perfect
for sparking conversations in your book
group or for digging deeper into the text
on your own.

www.bookclubhub.net

*You'll also find free discussion guides for
other Tyndale books, e-newsletters, e-mail
devotionals, virtual book tours, and more!*

TYNDALE